User Comments and Mo
in Digital Journalism

This book is an authoritative discussion of user comments and moderation in digital journalism, examining how user comments have disrupted the field of journalism and how a growing number of news organizations have abandoned commenting features altogether.

Making a broad argument concerning user commentary as a manifestation of user engagement and public deliberation, *User Comments and Moderation in Digital Journalism: Disruptive Engagement* conceptualizes the act of commenting as interactive engagement and participation in a virtual public sphere. The book also explores the organizational policies that have the potential to disrupt – as well as improve – the quality of user discussions. Ultimately, strategies are proposed for managing and improving user comments and encouraging more productive public deliberation in digital journalism.

This engaging discussion of a key development in digital journalism is a valuable resource for academics and researchers in the areas of journalism, media and communication studies.

Thomas B. Ksiazek holds a PhD from Northwestern University, USA, and is an associate professor in the Department of Communication at Villanova University, USA. His research interests include new forms of user engagement with the news, implications of audience behavior for society and the field of journalism, patterns of cross-platform media use, and the application of network analysis to the consumption and production of media.

Nina Springer (Dr. phil., LMU Munich, Germany) is an associate professor in the Journalism Department at Södertörn University, Stockholm, Sweden. Her research focuses on journalists-audience-interactions and the journalistic profession. In the realm of commentary features, she investigated commenters' motives and contributions to viewpoint diversity, as well as comments' use for and their effects on audiences and journalists alike.

Disruptions: Studies in Digital Journalism

Series editor: Bob Franklin

Disruptions refers to the radical changes provoked by the affordances of digital technologies that occur at a pace and on a scale that disrupts settled understandings and traditional ways of creating value, interacting and communicating both socially and professionally. The consequences for digital journalism involve far reaching changes to business models, professional practices, roles, ethics, products and even challenges to the accepted definitions and understandings of journalism. For Digital Journalism Studies, the field of academic inquiry which explores and examines digital journalism, disruption results in paradigmatic and tectonic shifts in scholarly concerns. It prompts reconsideration of research methods, theoretical analyses and responses (oppositional and consensual) to such changes, which have been described as being akin to 'a moment of mind-blowing uncertainty'.

Routledge's new book series, *Disruptions: Studies in Digital Journalism*, seeks to capture, examine and analyse these moments of exciting and explosive professional and scholarly innovation which characterize developments in the day-to-day practice of journalism in an age of digital media, and which are articulated in the newly emerging academic discipline of Digital Journalism Studies.

Hacking Gender and Technology in Journalism
Sara De Vuyst

New Media Unions
Nicole Cohen and Greig De Peuter

User Comments and Moderation in Digital Journalism
Thomas B. Ksiazek and Nina Springer

For more information, please visit: www.routledge.com/Disruptions/book-series/DISRUPTDIGJOUR

User Comments and Moderation in Digital Journalism

Disruptive Engagement

Thomas B. Ksiazek and Nina Springer

LONDON AND NEW YORK

First published 2020
by Routledge
2 Park Square, Milton Park, Abingdon, Oxon, OX14 4RN

and by Routledge
52 Vanderbilt Avenue, New York, NY 10017

Routledge is an imprint of the Taylor & Francis Group, an informa business

Library of Congress Cataloging-in-Publication Data
A catalog record for this title has been requested

ISBN: 978-0-367-22642-8 (hbk)
ISBN: 978-0-367-49752-1 (pbk)
ISBN: 978-0-429-27613-2 (ebk)

Typeset in Times New Roman
by codeMantra

Thomas B. Ksiazek
To my wife, Melinda, for her unwavering and loving support. To her and our two young children, Ty and Cora, for giving me the peace of mind and motivation—and sleep—I needed to write this book.

Nina Springer
To Eli. Achim, Annie, and Heidi—deeply grateful for all your support.

Contents

Illustrations

Figures

Tables

Acknowledgments

Thomas B. Ksiazek
To countless colleagues and students, both past and present. This work dates back a decade, to my time as a PhD student at Northwestern University. While embarking on a large-scale content analysis of YouTube news videos, my colleague Limor Peer suggested, "Why don't we capture these comments posted below the videos? There could be some interesting research opportunities there." And so, it began.

Limor and I published several studies and book chapters together, exploring user comments posted to YouTube news videos, some of which were co-authored with Kevin Lessard and Andrew Zivic, both graduate students at Villanova University. This laid the groundwork for the empirical research that serves as the foundation for much of this book. That work has been generously supported over the years by the Waterhouse Family Institute for the Study of Communication and Society at Villanova as well as multiple University Summer Grants and Summer Research Fellowships from Villanova. This research would also not have been possible without the tireless support of my dedicated undergraduate (Caroline Hroncich, Nicole Villegas) and graduate (Maria Nelson, Sri Varsha Devineni) research assistants.

Finally, I'd be remiss if I didn't acknowledge my co-author, Nina Springer. I've had the great honor of collaborating with such a smart and thoughtful colleague these past few years. It's been a true pleasure writing this book together.

Nina Springer
My academic career started with an interest in why people comment on news, and I feel I still haven't answered this conclusively for myself. However, I guess "the journey is the reward," and I am grateful that many students and colleagues were part of this journey, enriching it incredibly. I was blessed to have great guidance

and input along the way from the professors I worked with: Thomas Hanitzsch, Michael Meyen, Heinz Pürer, and Jens Wolling. Further, a lot of wonderfully curious and inquiring students found interest in the topic. I am grateful for all their smart thoughts and input. Here, a special "thank you" for the most awesome support goes out to Dunja Hoyh, Lisa Hemmerich, Moritz Baumstieger, Anna Sophie Kümpel, Ramona Ludolph, and Christian Pfaffinger—who contributed greatly in different contexts to my dissertation work. LMU Munich offers important financial resources for young female scholars, and I am thankful that I could tap into these throughout my PhD and Post-doc years. LMU's Department of Media and Communication also hosts some of the smartest and most inspiring people on earth. I had the honor to explore user comments not only with all the bright persons mentioned before but also with my incredible colleagues back then: Christian Baden, Ines Engelmann, Mario Haim (who also gave the chapter on machine learning in comment moderation a second look), and Benjamin Krämer. Furthermore, I was greatly inspired by collaborations with some of the most fantastic scholars: Gina Masullo Chen, Pablo Jost, Scott Wright, and Marc Ziegele. Finally, deep gratitude goes out to Tom B. Ksiazek. Not only did he invite me to depart on this endeavor—he also made me stand at the top of a skyscraper in Philadelphia. I must say, the feelings of submitting a book manuscript and surviving eye-to-eye contact with William Penn in Philadelphia's heavens are quite comparable. Journeys with Tom are inspiring, enriching, and wonderfully special—his clarity in thinking is legendary. What a pleasure to collaborate with such a great scholar and person.

1 Early and current debates on user commentary

The lack of civility and growing polarization in our discussion of politics is a public concern across the globe. For instance, while the vast majority of Americans (95.4%) recognize the importance of civility in politics for the health of democracy (Center for Political Participation, 2010, April 20), nearly as many Americans (91%) think "the lack of civility in politics today is a serious problem" (Quinnipiac University Poll, 2018, July 3), and 93% identify incivility as a general problem in society today (Weber Shandwick, 2019). Perhaps of most concern are trends indicating that Americans think the problem is getting worse: A plurality (49%) think that debate has become less civil (CBS News Poll, 2011, January 11), and a majority (74%) think our society is "ruder today" than it was 20–30 years ago (Associated Press/National Opinion Research Center, 2016, April 15). Similarly, 75% of Germans believe people were more polite in the past than they are today (YouGov, 2015), and more than three-fourths (78%) of German Internet users have already encountered online hate speech (Landesanstalt für Medien NRW, 2018). The internet and social media are typically held responsible for these developments (e.g., Weber Shandwick, 2019).

User comments in digital journalism (i.e., the discussions that occur in the spaces below digital news articles) are one place where incivility has received a great deal of attention and critical scrutiny—publicly, as well as in academic and industry communities. As users engage with digital forms of journalism in varied ways, the ability to immediately take part in a public discussion of current events with other, often anonymous, commenters has sparked widespread debates about the value and necessity of user comments. While user comments are celebrated for their potential to encourage public engagement and deliberation, at the same time they are widely criticized for their often uncivil nature. In many ways, user comments have disrupted the field of journalism, and a growing number of news organizations have abandoned their commenting features altogether.

The problematic public perception of disruptive user comments marks the "end for now" of a development that was polarizing from the very beginning.

The transmission of news via the Internet and the installment of such interactive features mostly between the 1990s and 2000s started a process of unprecedented audience presence in the journalists' working realm. Commenting features, as one of the most prominent formats for audience participation in the news production process (e.g., Hermida, 2011b, p. 180), resulted in thousands of user contributions per day for some major news outlets (e.g., Haim, Heinzel, Lankheit, Niagu, & Springer, 2019; Häring, Loosen, & Maalej, 2018; Hermida, 2011a, p. 25). And the stream continues to flow for those outlets that still allow the audience to comment on their content. However, the process of audience engagement via commenting features was and still is accompanied by "significant internal conflict among both journalists and readers" (Robinson, 2010, p. 125). Journalists who conceptualize a hierarchical relationship between them and their audiences (Sue Robinson calls them "traditionalists") clash with the ones who embrace and encourage options for audience participation on their news sites (in Robinson's conceptualization: "convergers"). In her ethnographic study, Robinson (2010) observed that "[t]hese categorical distinctions held true for readers as well," with some favoring journalistic engagement and moderation while others advocated "free rein" in these spaces (pp. 131, 137). Moreover, "stark differences emerged between journalists and their online contributors regarding generally held values for these spaces" (p. 131). The tone and style in which some users vented in the comment spaces, as illustrated above, are often in conflict with journalists' expectations of idealized user contributions on their sites; what newsroom staff see as quality contributions usually aligns with traditional journalistic standards (e.g., Diakopoulos, 2015; Robinson, 2010; Wolfgang, 2018). Lastly, a third group of stakeholders was found to have a quite polarized attitude toward user comments: readers who do not actively comment themselves. While some of these "lurkers" tend to find the comments informative and entertaining, others perceive user contributions as too uncivil and too poor in quality (e.g., Diakopoulos & Naaman, 2011; Springer, Engelmann, & Pfaffinger, 2015). Given these perceptions, it is unsurprising that journalists usually do not tend to see user comments as valuable contributions to the news production process (e.g., Hermida, 2011a, p. 25).

That process of news production in legacy media can be conceptualized across five stages (Domingo et al., 2008): Journalists gather information (access and observation stage) about issues that are selected for publication due to their attributed relevance and newsworthiness (selection and filtering stage), and they produce and edit their accounts (processing and editing stage) to disseminate them (distribution stage) so that they can subsequently be discussed publicly (interpretation stage) (see also Hermida, 2011a, p. 18). For traditional journalism, studies show that cooperation with users mostly happens during the access and observation and distribution stages: Users are oftentimes asked to submit story ideas and materials, such as eye-witness accounts, or to share articles within their social networks, respectively (e.g., Hermida, 2011b, p. 180; Larsson, 2012, p. 207). Within the selection and filtering as well as the processing and editing stages, however, users' direct involvement in editorial processes is usually kept at bay. One exception to this involves engaging commenters as "proofreaders" and instruments of quality control (e.g., Heinonen, 2011, pp. 42–43). Nevertheless, traditional journalists view the decision of news selection and presentation as the core of their professional work that has to be defended (e.g., Borger, Van Hoof, & Sanders, 2016; Domingo et al., 2008; Hermida, 2011a). Although the interpretation stage in traditional journalism around the globe is commonly seen as the most open stage for user participation and feedback (Hermida, 2011b, p. 180), journalists usually perceive user commentary as a conversation or a debate about what they have produced that happens "below the line" (Graham & Wright, 2015) after their job has been done (Hermida, 2011a, p. 25; Reich, 2011, p. 96).

While substantial direct influence of user commentary on journalistic production processes is thus considerably limited, it is plausible to assume that the amount, content, or sentiment of incoming user comments can have an indirect impact on journalistic selection and editing processes. Audience feedback is "informing journalists whether and how their products resonate with audiences and helping journalists see what needs to be done in future stories" (Heinonen, 2011, p. 40). Commenting users can be perceived as "sensors" for audience interests and "audience pulse-takers" as well as "reflectors" of the news; thereby they "serve as an important complement to other monitoring mechanisms, such as readership surveys and market analyses" (p. 41). While journalists generally acknowledge that experts are among commenters (p. 39), only very recently have some major news outlets and scholars started to explore ways for strategic retrievals of the comments' potential. The latest endeavors engage, for instance, in computational developments to automatically detect information in comments that can be used for journalistic purposes (e.g., Diakopoulos, 2015; Haim et al., 2019; Häring et al., 2018; Kolhatkar & Taboada, 2017; Napoles, Tetreault, Pappu, Rosato, & Provenzale, 2017; Park, Sachar, Diakopoulos, & Elmqvist, 2016). Such information can include arguments used by or personal stories of commenters to generate story ideas for follow-ups or all sorts of feedback on editorial or comment moderation processes (e.g., Schabus, Skowron, & Trapp, 2017).

Audience inclusion in journalism has been analyzed by means of different concepts in journalism studies, such as "participatory journalism" (e.g., Singer et al., 2011), "citizen journalism" (e.g., Chung, Nah, & Yamamoto, 2018), or "reciprocal journalism" (Lewis, Holton, & Coddington, 2014; similar ideas can be found in the concept of "journalism-as-a-conversation," see Marchionni, 2013). "Citizen journalism" is often applied to analyze "citizens engaging in journalistic activities outside the scope of professional organizations" (Borger et al., 2016, p. 711). The scope of this book, however, is *user commentary on professionally produced journalistic content.* Thus, "participatory" or "reciprocal" journalism provide more fitting conceptual frameworks for our endeavor. Traditionally, user comments on online news sites had been viewed as a form of "participatory journalism." In their seminal book on "participatory journalism," Singer et al. (2011) coined the understanding of this concept as capturing

> the idea of collaborative and collective – not simply parallel – action. People inside and outside the newsroom are engaged in communicating not only *to*, but also *with*, one another. In doing so, they all are participating in the ongoing processes of creating a news website and building a multifaceted community.
>
> (p. 2)

Building on this, a "reciprocal journalism" framework would conceptualize commenting features as a tool to foster reciprocal engagement between professional journalists and citizen contributors in a co-creation mindset, resulting in community building between journalists and users through more equal and longer-lasting relations (Lewis et al., 2014). While both concepts effectively capture commenting features' potential, we have to acknowledge (as already discussed) that user comments were as of yet generally not considered real contributions to the first stages of the journalistic news production process. Rather, audience members are invited or at least accepted to participate in the interpretation of news that had already been produced and published on the organizations' websites and the outlets' social media pages. Moreover, journalists as of yet oftentimes do not make use of these features to engage publicly in discussions with their audiences (e.g., Graham & Wright, 2015; Jakobs, 2014, p. 201). The advancements in computation, however, bear the potential to more efficiently identify and retrieve useful information from audience contributions and feed such elements into the news production routines. Thus, we might see more of the commenting features' participatory potential released in the future.

As with the concept of "reciprocal journalism" (or, similarly, "journalism-as-a-conversation"), the idea of "participatory journalism" comes with a fair share of normative load. "[A]t the origins of participatory journalism lie normative ideas that are inextricably linked with democracy, a core value of both journalism and journalism studies" (Borger, Van Hoof, Costera Meijer, & Sanders, 2013, p. 126). Every stage in the news production process demands decisions and thus selectivity—something that has always been subject to scholarly and "mainstream media" criticism. Thus, commenting features have been praised for their democratic potential: Through these interactive features, individuals in a civil society (neither organized nor rich in resources) are enabled to speak and discuss their viewpoints in public. Alternative interpretations to "elite" or "mainstream" frames can become visible, allowing societal self-observation to the smallest unities. Hence, scholars regularly conclude that the news organizations' daily duties are no longer limited to news detection, selection, production and distribution: Online news media have become platforms for public discourse (e.g., Braun & Gillespie, 2011). Understanding and engaging with users as contributors, and seeing their contributions as valuable input for decisions on the selection and presentation of topics would eventually allow for a democratization of the news production process. However, individual and strategic misuse of the commenting features have been reported: Not only have frequent incivility and the spread of hate speech raised concerns from the very beginning (e.g., Köffer, Riehle, Höhenberger, & Becker, 2018; Ksiazek, 2018; Santana, 2015), but the more recently observed concerted spread of (bought and fabricated) comments for political propaganda is similarly alarming (e.g., King, Pan, & Roberts, 2017; Lau, 2016; Schmookler, 2014; Sindelar, 2014).

Such problematic forms of user-generated contributions had led, early on, to the emergence of new job profiles such as "community manager" or "comment moderator." Due to their capacity of screening, selecting or editing user contributions, these roles signal a new category of gatekeeping actors (e.g., Hermida, 2011b; Paulussen, 2011) that might easily be perceived as "a pure censor's office" (Haim et al., 2019): "[F]ostering public discourse at times means moderating and silencing the voices of individuals, and conversely…managing a community must sometimes take a backseat to public obligation" (Braun & Gillespie, 2011, p. 394). Hence, the relationship between comment moderators and commenters is not always free of tensions (e.g., Springer, 2014). Moreover, the normative scholarly conceptions and their clash with empirical findings on the actual usage of commenting features marks another disruption that comes with this polarizing phenomenon.

In the subsequent chapters, we explore all of these disruptions mentioned in this introductory chapter. In doing so, we focus on comments posted to news outlets' websites, and mostly neglect work that has been conducted on user comments posted to social news sites such as Facebook, Twitter, or YouTube. The only overlap will be research on comments posted to Facebook pages of news outlets, but even this will be more cursory. The reasons behind this selectivity are:

- Given the scope of this book, we are primarily interested in how audiences engage with (digital) journalism. While journalism is notoriously hard to define (e.g., Shapiro, 2014), the most feasible workaround is to understand digital journalism in our context as informational content produced by professional journalists and published by online news sites.
- Compared to comments disseminated on social networking sites, user comments posted to these online news sites have an enormous potential reach, which gives them a significant potential to impact public opinion (e.g., Springer, 2014).
- Lastly, the phenomenon of "commenting on news" originally started in the wake of experimenting with interactive features on news sites. Such technical tools allow for journalist–citizen interaction (e.g., Marchionni, 2013). Shifting user commentary to social media pages is a recent trend in which the dissemination and interpretation stages are decoupled from the earlier stages of news production. Even organizationally, social media channels do not necessarily have to be fed by the journalistic department in a news outlet. Hence, the shift sets the participation hurdles higher (only those registered with the third-party platform are able to engage) and perceptibly increases the separation between the creative stages of the news production process and the interpretation stage, which is most open to audience participation.

From conceptualizing the act of commenting as both interactive engagement and participation in a virtual public sphere to exploring the organizational policies that, on the other hand, have the potential to disrupt—but also to improve—the quality of user discussions, our hope is that this book contributes the following to our understanding of the current state of user commentary in digital journalism:

- Conceptualizing user commentary and moderation as simultaneously disruptive forces in digital journalism. By taking on this perspective, we treat the phenomenon of user commentary holistically, and explore the experiences of newsrooms and users alike (instead of focusing on either the news outlets' or the users' experiences with commentary features).
- An expansive treatment of comment moderation, including the role of AI/machine learning, in the context of organizational policies for managing user commentary.
- Empirical and theoretical treatment of anonymity in commenting.
- Recognizing both the engagement and deliberative potential of user commentary for the field of journalism.
- A compilation and reframing of extensive empirical analysis, coupled with novel insights into public statements from news organizations explaining their logic for removing user comments from their websites. We should note that Ksiazek and Springer (2018), in particular, served as a foundation for this book (readers are encouraged to review that book chapter for a more concise treatment of many topics covered here).
- International scope, drawing on research conducted on news organizations and user commentary from all over the world, with a particular focus on the United States, Germany, and the United Kingdom.

In the following sections, we offer an overview on two key themes that we revisit throughout this book: (1) how comments represent a form of disruptive engagement for news professionals and organizations, and (2) how the moderation practices of those organizations can simultaneously serve as a disruptive presence for commenters.

Disruptive engagement

Increased user engagement has disrupted traditional power dynamics in the journalist-audience relationship, giving greater voice to users and more control over content appearing on digital news outlets. We situate comments as a form of disruptive user engagement, which is in turn disrupted by the moderation process enacted by news organizations. We theorize comments as a manifestation of user engagement with the news/journalists, each other, and/or the public. We also offer a conceptual model of engagement that understands commenting as simultaneously embodying cognitive, emotional and behavioral dimensions.

While not all forms of engagement across the news production process are disruptive in a negative sense (e.g., crowdsourced content and increased news distribution through user sharing can have positive impacts for news organizations), comments in particular are seen by journalists as uncivil and cumbersome to manage (e.g., Barnes, 2015; Goodman, 2013; Lee, 2012; Meltzer, 2015; Nielsen, 2012; Santana, 2011, 2014; Singer et al., 2011). Concerns about incivility in comments often emphasize a disruption in norms of deliberation about current events, and anonymity in comments contradicts ethical norms in journalism regarding transparency and source attribution.

Many news organizations have gone so far as to abandon their commenting features, or shift them to third-party social media platforms, despite the perceived deliberative potential of these discussions. To better understand these decisions, we conducted an analysis of recent public statements from news organizations about their rationale for removing comments. The results of this analysis shed light on the organizational reasoning for removing commenting features. Here, we offer a summary of these findings and return to a more detailed treatment in the concluding chapter.

Our analysis identified 20 news organizations that have recently suspended or abandoned the ability for users to comment on their articles. The results indicated that news organizations that chose to remove commenting functions had not only clear convictions about why the decision was necessary but also strong normative ideas about what commenting ought to look like. Though these organizations sometimes wrote passionately about the preservation and importance of the communities of online readership their websites had fostered, there was a widespread sentiment that removing comments from their platforms was part of a greater mission contributing to the improvement of information dissemination and the internet as a whole.

Concrete reasons as to why comments were being removed ranged from concerns about incivility; to the idea that bad commenters were skewing public perception of the news stories, scientific facts, or the news organization itself; to the protection of sensitive subjects, content, and the reputation of journalists. The analysis revealed extensive references to incivility as a reason for removing commentary functions. This language highlighted prejudicial statements, misogyny, racism, and more general abuse. Types of comments and commenters that were largely deemed as undesirable were often named as either trolls or spam/bots. Another bad commenting practice discussed in the statements was what the Guardian's Stephen Pritchard termed "author abuse" (Pritchard, 2016, March 26): Some statements framed the reasoning for removing comment sections as a way to take a stand against readers who share prejudicial sentiments specifically directed at journalists.

In sum, the analysis points to the perceived disruptive nature of user comments. It seems that for many news organizations, these concerns are deemed serious enough to abandon their commenting capabilities altogether. In the final chapter, we offer a more detailed treatment of this analysis as context for our discussion of whether news organizations should give up on managing user comments or look for ways to encourage more productive user engagement.

Disruptive moderation

Not only are user comments disruptive for newsrooms, but comment moderators' gatekeeping acts of policing and banning contributions impact the development and the course of user discussions. Comment moderation can be perceived as newsroom censorship from the user perspective, and a lack of transparency about moderation and/or sensitive moderation rules can be perceived as being disruptive to user discussions.

According to relevant literature in participatory journalism studies (Singer, 2011; Wolfgang, 2018), moderators can be seen as new gatekeeping actors, deciding whether comments are publishable, and therefore whether or not certain opinions are acceptable. Setting aside legally problematic content, decisions regarding publishable/acceptable comments constitute a gray area, which is only negotiable between moderators and users if the moderators are open to such conversations and to revisions of their decisions (certainly depending on resources and moderators' attitudes and role conceptions). Related, the recent trend toward implementing AI/machine learning moderation tools has introduced new algorithmic gatekeepers in the moderation process. Since moderators—supported by algorithms—always have the final say, they exercise power over commenters.

Current debates

The subsequent chapters are organized around the most compelling current debates on the state of user commentary in digital journalism. Chapter 2 conceptualizes user commentary as a form of interactive engagement with digital journalism. Here, we situate comments as part of a broader trend toward increased user participation, interaction, and engagement with the news. Next, we lay out our conceptual model of engagement, drawing on previous work that synthesizes the myriad, disparate understandings of user engagement. The model argues that engagement is a relative combination of psychological (cognitive/emotional) and behavioral dimensions, and indicators of engagement exist along a continuum from low to high engagement. We discuss how commenting simultaneously embodies cognitive, emotional and behavioral aspects of engagement, and we also situate commenting along a continuum from low (e.g., reading) to high (e.g., commenting) engagement with the news. Next, we propose a Thread Structure Model that focuses on comments as a particular manifestation of user engagement within virtual communities. We conclude this chapter by profiling commenters on demography and traits and discuss common motivators and inhibitors to commenting.

The third chapter draws on theories concerning the public sphere and deliberative democracy to understand comments as a form of public engagement and to contextualize our analysis of (in)civility, viewpoint diversity, political action, and anonymity in user comments. This framework draws on Habermas's (1989) notion of the public sphere, a space where the public can engage in rational, civil discussion about the important events and issues of the day. Unfortunately, while both journalists and the general public seem to recognize the deliberative potential in commenting platforms, there is widespread concern about the quality of discussion occurring in these spaces. This chapter integrates our empirical and theoretical work on (in)civility in user comments (Ksiazek, 2015, 2018; Ksiazek & Peer, 2016; Ksiazek, Peer, & Zivic, 2015; Ksiazek & Springer, 2018), viewpoint diversity, comments as political action, and commenting effects (Baden & Springer, 2014; Ksiazek & Springer, 2018; Springer & Kümpel, 2018). We conclude this chapter by considering variations in commenting norms, beyond a traditional deliberation framework.

The fourth chapter engages the current debate around anonymity in user comments. Anonymity disrupts digital journalism by contradicting ethical norms in journalism regarding transparency and source attribution. Anonymous commenters are often blamed for the apparent pervasiveness of incivility in comments, and many news organizations now require commenters to be identifiable. We elaborate on the connection between anonymity and an "online disinhibition effect" (Suler, 2004, 2005), whereby if internet users can communicate anonymously, they can decouple their online and in-person actions and identities and thus "feel less vulnerable about self-disclosing or acting out" online (Suler, 2005, p. 185; see also Joinson, 2007). In this chapter, we also offer varying perspectives and organizational approaches to anonymity and integrate our empirical work on the relationships between anonymity and both user engagement and (in)civility.

The fifth chapter draws on our academic empirical research to inform applied organizational practices. We begin by outlining organizational perspectives on commenting and the relevant commenting policies put in place by news organizations to manage user comments. We review empirical analysis to offer insights into which organizational commenting policies encourage more engagement (volume of comments) and better quality comments (i.e., more civil/less hostile) (Ksiazek, 2015, 2018). In a critical reflection that follows, we shed light on the moderators' gatekeeping role and how this implemented power structure can impact the flow and content of user discussions. Given the widespread attention and varied implementation of comment moderation strategies, we devote a substantial portion of this chapter to the practical ways in which both organizations and users, themselves, moderate these discussion spaces. Finally, we conclude with a discussion of the current state of automation in comment moderation (artificial intelligence/machine learning).

The final chapter begins by returning to our focus on user commentary as disruptive engagement, asking whether the field of digital journalism should abandon comments (as some organizations have done) or find ways to encourage more productive commentary by critically assessing and reflecting on currently insufficient moderation strategies (e.g., those that are focused on policing and banning instead of being engaging and encouraging). We advocate for the latter position, returning to reflect on each of the current debates in the preceding chapters. In this final chapter, we explore organizational reasoning for abandoning comments as a backdrop and then propose an Integrated Comment Moderation Model that combines user-driven moderation, organizational policies and procedures, and innovative AI/machine learning tools. Our hope is that by adopting this type of approach, organizations and users can collectively encourage more productive commentary and mitigate the disruptions that have come to characterize how both news professionals and users perceive the user commentary process.

References

Associated Press/National Opinion Research Center Poll. (2016, April 15). *Associated Press.* Retrieved from http://www.orspub.com/document.php?id=quest16.out_1207&type=hitlist&num=30

Baden, C., & Springer, N. (2014). Com(ple)menting the news on the financial crisis: The contribution of news users' commentary to the diversity of viewpoints in the public debate. *European Journal of Communication, 29*(5), 529–548. doi: 10.1177/0267323114538724

Barnes, R. (2015). Understanding the affective investment produced through commenting on Australian alternative journalism website New Matilda. *New Media & Society, 17*(5), 810–826. doi: 10.1177/1461444813511039

Borger, M., Van Hoof, A., Costera Meijer, I., & Sanders, J. (2013). Constructing participatory journalism as a scholarly object: A genealogical analysis. *Digital Journalism, 1*(1), 117–134. doi: 10.1080/21670811.2012.740267

Borger, M., Van Hoof, A., & Sanders, J. (2016). Expecting reciprocity: Towards a model of the participants' perspective on participatory journalism. *New Media & Society, 18*(5), 708–725. doi: 10.1177/1461444814545842

Braun, J., & Gillespie, T. (2011). Hosting the public discourse, hosting the public: When online news and social media converge. *Journalism Practice, 5*(4), 383–398. doi: 10.1080/17512786.2011.557560

CBS News Poll. (2011, January 11). *CBS News.* Retrieved from http://www.orspub.com/document.php?id=quest11.out_2191&type=hitlist&num=48

Center for Political Participation Poll. (2010, April 20). *Center for Political Participation.* Retrieved from http://www.orspub.com/document.php?id=quest10.out_1602&type=hitlist&num=52

Chung, D. S., Nah, S., & Yamamoto, M. (2018). Conceptualizing citizen journalism: US news editors' views. *Journalism, 19*(12), 1694–1712. doi: 10.1177/1464884916686596

Diakopoulos, N. (2015). Picking the NYT Picks: Editorial criteria and automation in the curation of online news comments. *ISOJ Journal, 6*(1), 147–166.

Diakopoulos, N., & Naaman, M. (2011). Towards quality discourse in online news comments. *Proceedings of CSCW 2011* (pp. 133–142). March 19–23, Hangzhou, China. doi: 10.1145/1958824.1958844

Domingo, D., Quandt, T., Heinonen, A., Paulussen, S., Singer, J. B., & Vujnovic, M. (2008). Participatory journalism practices in the media and beyond: An international comparative study of initiatives in online newspapers. *Journalism Practice, 2*(3), 326–342. doi: 10.1080/17512780802281065

Goodman, E. (2013). Online comment moderation: Emerging best practices. *World Association of Newspapers (WAN-IFRA).* Retrieved from http://www.wan-ifra.org/reports/2013/10/04/online-comment-moderation-emerging-best-practices.

Graham, T., & Wright, S. (2015). A tale of two stories from "Below the Line" comment fields at the Guardian. *The International Journal of Press/Politics, 20*(3), 317–338. doi: 10.1177/1940161215581926

Habermas, J. (1989). *The structural transformation of the public sphere: An inquiry into a category of bourgeois society*. Cambridge, MA: MIT Press.

Haim, M., Heinzel, I., Lankheit, S., Niagu, A. M., & Springer, N. (2019, May). *Identifying the good and the bad: Using machine learning to moderate user commentary on news*. Paper presentation at the annual International Communication Association (ICA) conference, Washington, DC.

Häring, M., Loosen, W., & Maalej, W. (2018). Who is addressed in this comment? Automatically classifying meta-comments in news comments. *Proceedings of the ACM on Human-Computer Interaction*. November 3–7, New York. doi: 10.1145/3274336

Heinonen, A. (2011). The journalist's relationship with users. New dimensions to conventional roles. In J. B. Singer, A. Hermida, D. Domingo, A. Heinonen, S. Paulussen, T. Quandt, … (Eds.), *Participatory journalism. Guarding open gates at online newspapers* (pp. 34–55). Sussex: Wiley-Blackwell.

Hermida, A. (2011a). Mechanisms of participation: How audience options shape the conversation. In J. B. Singer, A. Hermida, D. Domingo, A. Heinonen, S. Paulussen, T. Quandt, … (Eds.), *Participatory journalism. Guarding open gates at online newspapers* (pp. 13–33). Sussex: Wiley-Blackwell.

Hermida, A. (2011b). Fluid spaces, fluid journalism. The role of the "Active Recipient" in participatory journalism. In J. B. Singer, A. Hermida, D. Domingo, A. Heinonen, S. Paulussen, T. Quandt, … (Eds.), *Participatory journalism. Guarding open gates at online newspapers* (pp. 177–191). Sussex: Wiley-Blackwell.

Jakobs, I. (2014). Diskutieren für mehr Demokratie? Zum deliberativen Potenzial von Leserkommentaren zu journalistischen Texten im Internet. In W. Loosen & M. Dohle (Eds.), *Journalismus und (sein) Publikum* (pp. 191–210). Wiesbaden: Springer.

Joinson, A. N. (2007). Disinhibition and the Internet. In J. Gackenbach (Ed.), *Psychology and the internet. Intrapersonal, interpersonal, and transpersonal implications* (2nd ed., pp. 75–92). San Diego: Academic Press.

King, G., Pan, J., & Roberts, M. E. (2017). How the Chinese government fabricates social media posts for strategic distraction, not engaged argument. *American Political Science Review, 111*(3), 484–501. doi: 10.1017/S0003055417000144

Köffer, S., Riehle, D. M., Höhenberger, S., & Becker, J. (2018). Discussing the value of automatic hate speech detection in online debates. Paper presented at the *Multikonferenz Wirtschaftsinformatik (MKWI 2018): Data Driven X-Turning Data in Value*. Leuphana, Germany. March 6–9.

Kolhatkar, V., & Taboada, M. (2017). Using New York Times picks to identify constructive comments. *Proceedings of the 2017 EMNLP Workshop: Natural Language Processing meets Journalism* (pp. 100–105). September, Copenhagen, Denmark. doi: 10.18653/v1/W17-42

Ksiazek, T. B. (2015). Civil interactivity: How news organizations' commenting policies explain civility and hostility in user comments. *Journal of Broadcasting & Electronic Media, 59*(4), 556–573. doi: 10.1080/08838151.2015.1093487

Ksiazek, T. B. (2018). Commenting on the news: Explaining the degree and quality of user comments on news websites. *Journalism Studies, 19*(5), 650–673. doi: 10.1080/1461670X.2016.1209977

Ksiazek, T. B., & Peer, L. (2016). User comments and civility on YouTube. In B. Franklin & S.A. Eldridge II (Eds.), *Routledge companion to digital journalism studies* (pp. 244–252). New York: Routledge.

Ksiazek, T. B., Peer, L., & Zivic, A. (2015). Discussing the news: Civility and hostility in user comments. *Digital Journalism, 3*(6), 850–870, doi: 10.1080/21670811.2014.972079

Ksiazek, T. B., & Springer, N. (2018). User comments in digital journalism: Current research and future directions. In S. A. Eldridge II & B. Franklin (Eds.), *Routledge handbook of developments in digital journalism studies* (pp. 475–486). London, New York: Routledge.

Landesanstalt für Medien NRW (2018). Forsa-Befragung zur Wahrnehmung von Hassrede im Internet. Retrieved from https://www.medienanstalt-nrw.de/foerderung/forschung/abgeschlossene-projekte/forsa-befragung-zur-wahrnehmung-von-hassrede.html

Larsson, A. O. (2012). Interactivity on Swedish newspaper websites: What kind, how much and why? *Convergence: The International Journal of Research into New Media Technologies, 18*(2), 195–213. doi: 10.1177/1354856511430184

Lau, J. (2016, 7 October). Who are the Chinese trolls of the '50 Cent Army'? *Voice of America*. Retrieved from https://www.voanews.com/east-asia-pacific/who-are-chinese-trolls-50-cent-army

Lee, E. J. (2012). That's not the way it is: How user-generated comments on the news affect perceived media bias. *Journal of Computer-Mediated Communication, 18*(1), 32–45. doi: 10.1111/j.1083-6101.2012.01597.x

Lewis, S. C., Holton, A. E., & Coddington, M. (2014). Reciprocal journalism: A concept of mutual exchange between journalists and audiences. *Journalism Practice, 8*(2), 229–241. doi: 10.1080/17512786.2013.859840

Marchionni, D. M. (2013). Journalism-as-a-conversation: A concept explication. *Communication Theory, 23*(2), 131–147. doi: 10.1111/comt.12007

Meltzer, K. (2015). Journalistic concern about uncivil political talk in digital news media: Responsibility, credibility, and academic influence. *The International Journal of Press/Politics, 20*(1), 85–107. doi: 10.1177/1940161214558748

Napoles, C., Tetreault, J., Pappu, A., Rosato, E., & Provenzale, B. (2017). Finding good conversations online: The Yahoo News Annotated Comments Corpus. *Proceedings of the 11th Linguistic Annotation Workshop*, EACL (pp. 13–23). April, Valencia, Spain. doi: 10.18653/v1/W17-0802

Nielsen, C. E. (2012). Newspaper journalists support online comments. *Newspaper Research Journal, 33*(1), 86–100. doi: 10.1177/073953291203300107

Park, D., Sachar, S., Diakopoulos, N., & Elmqvist, N. (2016, May). Supporting comment moderators in identifying high quality online news comments. *Proceedings of the 2016 CHI Conference on Human Factors in Computing Systems* (pp. 1114–1125). May 7–12, San Jose, CA. ACM. doi: 10.1145/2858036.2858389

Paulussen, S. (2011). Inside the newsroom. Journalists' motivations and organizational structures. In J. B. Singer, A. Hermida, D. Domingo, A. Heinonen, S. Paulussen, T. Quandt, … (Eds.), *Participatory journalism. Guarding open gates at online newspapers* (pp. 59–75). Sussex: Wiley-Blackwell.

Pritchard, S. (2016, March 26). The readers' editor on…closing comments below the line. *The Guardian*. Retrieved from https://www.theguardian.com/commentisfree/2016/mar/27/readers-editor-on-closing-com</ds> ments-below-line

Quinnipiac University Poll. (2018, July 3). *Quinnipiac University Polling Institute*. Retrieved from https://poll.qu.edu/national/release-detail?ReleaseID=2554

Reich, Z. (2011). User comments. The transformation of participatory space. In J. B. Singer, A. Hermida, D. Domingo, A. Heinonen, S. Paulussen, T. Quandt, … (Eds.), *Participatory journalism. Guarding open gates at online newspapers* (pp. 96–117). Sussex: Wiley-Blackwell.

Robinson, S. (2010). Traditionalists vs. convergers: Textual privilege, boundary work, and the journalist—Audience relationship in the commenting policies of online news sites. *Convergence: The International Journal of Research into New Media Technologies, 16*(1), 125–143. doi: 10.1177/1354856509347719

Santana, A. D. (2011). Online readers' comments represent new opinion pipeline. *Newspaper Research Journal, 32*(3), 66–81. doi: 10.1177/073953291103200306

Santana, A. D. (2014). Virtuous or vitriolic. The effect of anonymity on civility in online newspaper reader comment boards. *Journalism Practice, 8*(1), 18–33. doi: 10.1080/17512786.2013.813194

Santana, A. D. (2015). Incivility dominates online comments on immigration. *Newspaper Research Journal, 36*(1), 92–107. doi: 10.1177/0739532915580317

Schabus, D., Skowron, M., & Trapp, M. (2017). One million posts: A data set of German online discussions. *Proceedings of the 40th International ACM SIGIR Conference on Research and Development in Information Retrieval (SIGIR)* (pp. 1241–1244). August 7–11, Tokyo, Japan. doi: 10.1145/3077136.3080711

Schmookler, A. (2014, 2 Oct). The right-wing trolls have a strategy. What's ours? *Huffpost*. Retrieved from https://www.huffpost.com/entry/to-engage-with-rightwing-_b_5908346?guccounter=1&guce_referrer=aHR0cHM6Ly93d3cuZ29vZ2xlLmNvbS8&guce_referrer_sig=AQAAANUJAm-F1ECClxG2Mivx0x0zf7KSFVW57LQ9tL2loWko_2n508gd-hCW0sRs7jwssngXWCKvdPUMY0J6sN3OaGeadG_1wxcjd5K9A0vmD-Tdf9zZ-rhi_Mnjmo-nleNDeKbEbv6x8VIUG4dWYBNlFFtYEH7idxQqHDFmHpX_5Ug4

Shapiro, I. (2014). Why democracies need a functional definition of journalism now more than ever. *Journalism Studies, 15*(5), 555–565. doi: 10.1080/1461670X.2014.882483

Sindelar, D. (2014, 12 August). The Kremlin's Troll Army. Moscow is financing legions of pro-Russia Internet commenters. But how much do they matter? *The Atlantic*. Retrieved from https://www.theatlantic.com/international/archive/2014/08/the-kremlins-troll-army/375932/

Singer, J. B. (2011). Taking responsibility. Legal and ethical issues in participatory journalism. In J. B. Singer, A. Hermida, D. Domingo, A. Heinonen, S. Paulussen, T. Quandt, … (Eds.), *Participatory journalism. Guarding open gates at online newspapers* (pp. 121–138). Sussex: Wiley-Blackwell.

Singer, J. B., Hermida, A., Domingo, D., Heinonen, A., Paulussen, S., Quandt, T., …, & Vujnovic, M. (Eds.). (2011). *Participatory journalism. Guarding open gates at online newspapers.* Sussex: Wiley-Blackwell.

Springer, N. (2014). *Beschmutzte Öffentlichkeit? Warum Menschen die Kommentarfunktion auf Online-Nachrichtenseiten als öffentliche Toilettenwand benutzen, warum Besucher ihre Hinterlassenschaften trotzdem lesen, und wie die Wände im Anschluss aussehen.* LIT Verlag Münster.

Springer, N., Engelmann, I., & Pfaffinger, C. (2015). User comments: Motives and inhibitors to write and read. *Information, Communication & Society, 18*(7), 798–815. doi: 10.1080/1369118X.2014.997268

Springer, N., & Kümpel, A. (2018). User-generated (Dis)Content. Eine Literatursynopse zur Nutzung der Kommentarfunktion auf Online Nachrichtenseiten. In C. Nuernbergk & C. Neuberger (Eds.), *Journalismus im Internet: Profession – Partizipation – Technisierung* (pp. 241–271). 2. Auflage. Wiesbaden: VS.

Suler, J. (2004). The online disinhibition effect. *Cyberpsychology & Behavior, 7*(3), 321–326. doi: 10.1089/1094931041291295

Suler, J. (2005). The online disinhibition effect. *International Journal of Applied Psychoanalytic Studies, 2*(2), 184–188. doi: 10.1002/aps.42

Weber Shandwick. (2019). Civility in America 2019: Solutions for tomorrow. *Weber Shandwick We Solve.* Retrieved from https://www.webershandwick.com/wp-content/uploads/2019/06/CivilityInAmerica2019SolutionsforTomorrow.pdf

Wolfgang, J. D. (2018). Cleaning up the "fetid swamp:" Examining how journalists construct policies and practices for moderating comments. *Digital Journalism, 6*(1), 21–40. doi: 10.1080/21670811.2017.1343090

YouGov (2015, April 20). Haben die Deutschen ihre Manieren verloren? Retrieved from https://yougov.de/news/2015/04/20/generationen-sind-sich-einig-sachen-hoflichkeit/

2 Comments as engagement with the news

User comments, as a form of public engagement with the news, are often treated as the natural digital evolution of letters to the editor. For centuries, letters to the editor have offered newspaper readers an opportunity to participate in journalism by sharing their feedback with newspaper editors. In fact, Bill Reader (2015), in his expansive treatment of the history of audience feedback in the news media, dates letters to the editor to at least the 17th century.

User comments would rightly fall under a broader umbrella category of audience feedback, which would also include various metrics used to capture user behavior, along with other forms of feedback like letters to the editor. Yet the digital and interactive nature of user comments distinguishes them as a unique form of user engagement with the news. As we argue in this chapter, user comments simultaneously embody cognitive/emotional/behavioral aspects of user engagement; can range from low to high engagement along a continuum; can involve user-content reactions, user-user interactions, and/or user-journalist interactions; and constitute the core of a broader Thread Structure Model.

As the digital news environment becomes increasingly complex and competitive, news organizations have responded to a heightened sense of uncertainty in the marketplace by adopting policies that involve close monitoring of user behavior to inform organizational practices (Lowrey & Woo, 2010). Just as digital journalism is becoming increasingly data-driven, news organizations are adapting to be more responsive to the wealth of audience information available (e.g., Anderson, 2011; Arenberg & Lowrey, 2019; Ferrucci, 2018; Hanusch & Tandoc Jr., 2019; Lowrey & Woo, 2010; Nelson, 2019; Petre, 2015). While basic measures of exposure and popularity (e.g., ratings and circulation figures) have always been part of the audience valuation equation across media industries, we are seeing a shift from exposure-based metrics to engagement-based metrics to understand user behavior.

User engagement is a complex, even messy, term. Across fields, disciplines and industries, both scholars and practitioners have struggled to find consensus on what it means to engage with media or engage with an organizational entity vis-à-vis media (Hollebeek, 2011; Napoli, 2011; Nelson, 2019). In digital journalism, user engagement includes audience activities ranging from media exposure (e.g., time-spent on site, average page views, return visits), to publicly sharing an appreciation or preference for certain content (e.g., liking, sharing, recommending), to interacting with content more directly through commenting.

Most news organizations capture engagement through what Napoli (2011) calls a "basket of currencies" approach. This involves integrating various engagement metrics in comprehensive, customized models. To illustrate one such approach, Beckett (2010) revealed the engagement equation adopted from Peterson and Carabis (2008) and previously used by Philly.com, a joint digital venture of *The Philadelphia Inquirer* and *Philadelphia Daily News*. That equation, while no longer used by Philly.com, captured engagement through many common metrics still used today. These include: page views, time-spent on site, return visits (both frequency and recency), traffic source (e.g., direct traffic vs. search referrals), user-generated content contributions, and interactions through commenting. Table 2.1 offers a more generalized

Table 2.1 Common engagement metrics

Cognitive	*Emotional*	*Behavioral*
• Awareness • Recall	• Positive/negative sentiment • Interest/appreciation • Physiological response • Brand/organizational perception	• Comments and other forms of user-generated contributions • Time-spent/gaze time/gaze rate • Loyalty/recency (return visits) • Bounce-rate/average page views • Total interactions/ interaction rate/interaction time • Clicks/click-through rate/taps/swipes • Video completion • Social (likes, follows, shares, recommendations)

Adapted from Ksiazek (2018b); IAB (2014).

list of commonly used engagement metrics. These are organized across the three types of engagement discussed in our conceptual model below: cognitive, emotional, and behavioral. Most customized models involve some combination of these metrics to capture user engagement.

Although comments rarely have a direct impact on the news production process and the news product (see Chapter 1), they can have indirect effects on journalistic work processes since they help journalists understand users' interests and concerns (Hermida, 2011a, p. 25). User interests are no longer measured only by click rates and dwell time. Instead, by integrating both quantitative and qualitative feedback through user comments into the engagement equation, news outlets can immediately see reactions to articles, topics, and the manner in which they are presented.

In this chapter, we begin by introducing our conceptual model of engagement that synthesizes the myriad, disparate understandings of user engagement. The model argues that engagement is a relative combination of psychological (cognitive/emotional) and behavioral dimensions, and indicators of engagement exist along a continuum from low to high engagement. We discuss how commenting simultaneously embodies cognitive, emotional, and behavioral aspects of engagement, and we also situate commenting along a continuum from low (e.g., reading) to high (e.g., commenting) engagement with the news. Next, we propose a "Thread Structure Model" to situate commenting as a process that is initially motivated by news content and/or other comments and is iteratively moderated by news organizations, other users, and—increasingly—algorithms. We conclude the chapter by profiling commenters on demography and traits and discuss common motivations and inhibitors to commenting.

Conceptual model of engagement

When conceptualizing engagement, the literature categorizes dimensions of engagement, most often distinguishing between cognitive, emotional, and behavioral engagement (Brodie, Ilic, Juric, & Hollebeek, 2013; Hollebeek, 2011; Hollebeek, Glynn, & Brodie, 2014; IAB, 2014; Vivek, Beatty, & Morgan, 2012), as well as arguing that engagement is best understood along a continuum, generally moving from activities that signify less to more involvement or intensity (Ksiazek, Peer, & Lessard, 2014; Malthouse, Haenlein, Skiera, Wege, & Zhang, 2013; Napoli, 2011; Vivek et al., 2012). Our conceptual model integrates both psychological (cognitive/emotional) and behavioral dimensions of engagement, and conceptualizes engagement along a continuum (see Figure 2.1).

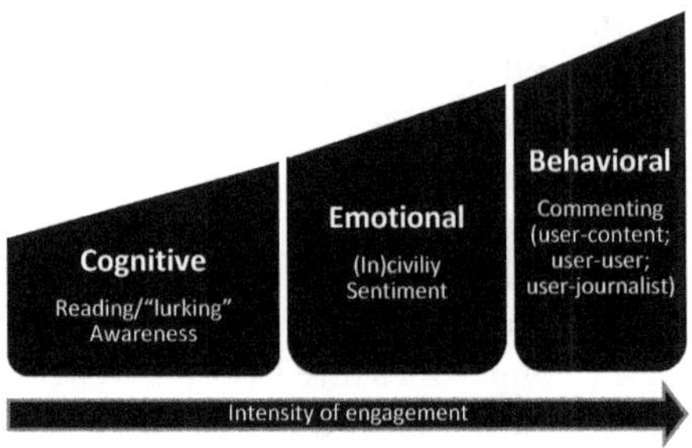

Figure 2.1 Conceptual model of user engagement.

Commenting, as a specific manifestation of user behavior, can be simultaneously indicative of cognitive, emotional, and behavioral user engagement. The act of commenting, itself, constitutes behavioral interaction with a news outlet and/or its other users. But commentary also inherently signals awareness—cognitive engagement—of the content on which a user is commenting and/or other comments to which a user is replying. Additionally, emotional engagement is often captured by user sentiment/tone toward content and other comments. Text mining, sentiment analysis, and other automated content analytic tools offer opportunities to capture emotional qualities of user commentary (e.g., positive/negative sentiment; (in)civility).

The engagement continuum in Figure 2.1 is underpinned by assumptions about the degree of cognitive and emotional intensity associated with a particular action. The act of reading comments, typically referred to as "lurking," is a lower intensity activity. While lurking can involve varying degrees of internal cognitive and emotional reactions to others' comments, the absence of acting on those reactions relegates lurkers to the lower end of the engagement continuum. The intensity of engagement increases when emotions are triggered in the reading process. Alternatively, posting a public comment in response to the content of an article or other users' comments signifies a higher level of engagement (Picone et al., 2019). This act requires cognitive/emotional reflection on the content/comments and then behavioral engagement via posting an actual comment for public consumption.

Behavioral engagement via commenting can range from *user-content reaction*, which involves a user interacting with content, such as posting an initial comment in response to an article. Alternatively, *user-user interaction* consists of interactions among two or more users, such as a user replying to another comment already posted to a thread by a different user (Ksiazek et al., 2014). Finally, *user-journalist interaction* involves both journalists participating in comment sections and users addressing journalists in their comments.

Thread Structure Model

Building on this user engagement model, it is useful to situate user commentary, in particular, within a *Thread Structure Model* (see Figure 2.2). In this model, news content is the initial stimulus that motivates cognitive/emotional engagement, which manifests as behavioral engagement via commenting. Since each comment thread on a news website is attached to a particular item of news content (e.g., article or video), it is reasonable to assume that comments are reactions to either the content (user-content reaction), other users' comments (user-user interaction), or the journalists themselves (user-journalist interaction).

While some user-user interaction involves users engaging with another person (dialogue), others engage by directing their comments toward a larger group of people (discussion). It is important to

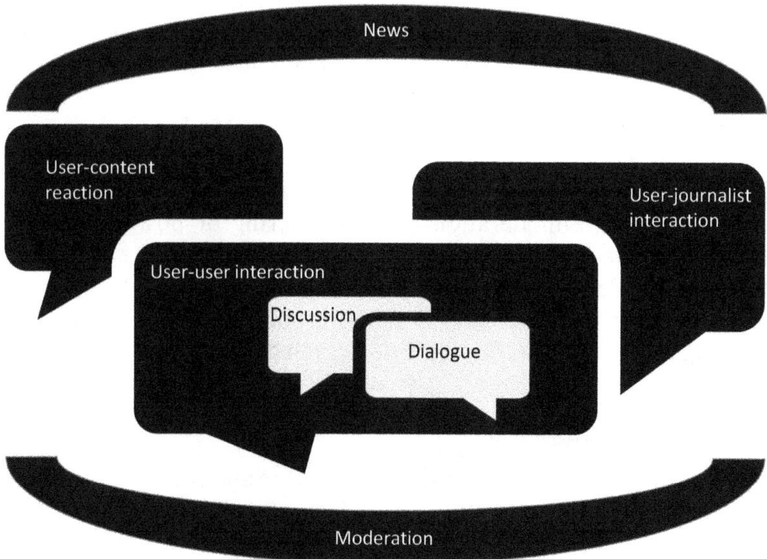

Figure 2.2 Thread Structure Model.

recognize that at this point, the news article may no longer be the focus of comments, as conversations may evolve beyond the original focus of the article. Existing research suggests that interactivity (comprising both dialogue and discussion) is affected by commenter- and comment-inherent factors but also impeded or facilitated externally through contextual factors. Focusing on the inherent factors, user-user interactivity is enabled through respective *motivations* that drive users to comment, e.g. the desire to discuss and exchange with others (Springer, Engelmann, & Pfaffinger, 2015; see the passage on "motivations and inhibitors" below). Since motives shape actions, such motivations should lead to a specific *style of commenting*. As research shows, comments will be more likely to engage others if they include controversial statements/topics, provide a different (unexpected) perspective, address others to emphasize a comment's relevance to them, ask questions, avoid extreme brevity, exclusively negative tone, and irony or metaphors for the sake of comprehensibility (Ksiazek, 2018a; Ziegele, Breiner, & Quiring, 2014, pp. 1127–1129). Furthermore, user-user-interactive comments were found to contain more arguments, be more fact-oriented and less emotional than user-content-reactive comments (Jakobs, 2014, pp. 204–205). As for external contextual factors, the *topic of the news item* itself was found to impact interactivity levels in comment sections (e.g., Ziegele et al., 2014). Further factors that we will discuss in the following section are the (*size of the*) *community* in which the activity of commenting is embedded (and which is impacted by factors such as the *outlet's reach* or *access requirements*), the *website architecture*, and *comment moderation*.

The last component of the Thread Structure Model involves management of user comments via moderation (which will be discussed in depth in Chapter 5). Comment moderation is enacted by organizations (e.g., pre-moderation through filtering or post-moderation through retroactive removal of comments), users (e.g., reporting or flagging hostile comments), and algorithms (e.g., profanity filters or machine learning approaches to support moderators' decisions in approving, promoting, and/or removing comments).

Commenting and communities

News organizations provide the infrastructure and thus virtual spaces for commentary, so that threads—which are oftentimes exclusively driven by commenters' activities—can evolve. To describe the commenters' virtual get-together and its management, literature, media practitioners, and the public discourse often refer to the terms "communities" and "community management." Comment spaces on news outlets enable the establishment of communities, however probably only "loosely knit ones" (Watson, Peng, & Lewis, 2019, p. 1843).

Commenters' get-togethers can be conceptualized as virtual communities insomuch as these *can* comprise "an aggregation of individuals...who interact around a shared interest, where the interaction is at least partially supported and/or mediated by technology and guided by some protocols or norms" (Porter, 2004; see also Watson et al., 2019). However, even a particular design for interaction "does not necessarily result in interactivity" (Porter, 2004): The "notion of community implies both something structural (e.g. a bounded location) and something socio-psychological (e.g. a sense of shared values developed through interaction with members)" (ibid.). Thus, the building and maintaining of a community not only require the news outlets' provision of a virtual meeting space but also involve processes on the users' side, such as "membership, inclusion, identity, feeling of belonging, and an emotional bond or sense of community..." (Wiesenfeld, 1996, p. 337, though critically engaging with these criteria). Accordingly, a construct to capture the "sense of virtual community" was found to be an important predictor of user participation in a study by Meyer and Carey (2014, pp. 221–222). Research in the area of community psychology on how people develop such a "sense of community" emphasizes that important indicators are the actual, planned, or anticipated "length of residency, home ownership, and satisfaction with the community" (McMillan & Chavis, 1986, p. 8). These ideas can be transferred to the building and maintaining of virtual communities: a user community that engages on news outlets' websites should develop and prevail if commenters establish long-term connections with the news site and reciprocal connections with each other; take ownership over the comment space; and, eventually, are satisfied with its state (see also Lewis, Holton, & Coddington, 2014; Watson et al., 2019).

In comment spaces, connections with each other are primarily established through user-user interaction (Figure 2.2). A comparative study found homogeneously fed comment spaces on some sites in which users rarely contribute more than one comment and seldomly interact with others, while other sites exhibited "communities of debate" that are "based on mostly respectful discussions between diverse points of view" (Ruiz et al., 2011, p. 463). Other studies also reported that shares of interactive comments and reciprocity in commenting vary considerably between news sites and platforms—from under 10% to over two-thirds (e.g., Canter, 2013; Esau, Friess, & Eilders, 2017; Graham & Wright, 2015; Jakobs, 2014; Slavtcheva-Petkova,

2016; Springer & Nuernbergk, 2016; Taddicken & Bund, 2010). High levels of user-user-interactivity had been measured, for example, for the German news outlet Spiegel Online (Jakobs, 2014; see also Springer, 2014; Ziegele et al., 2014). That outlet is among the most read news platforms in Germany, has a reputation for scrutinizing and acting as a "stronghold of democracy," and was among the first news magazines worldwide to go online in the 1990s (Spiegel, n.d.). Users' participation is organized by means of a forum design (Singer et al., 2011, pp. 198–199; Springer, 2014). Spiegel Online (SPON) publishes approximately 1.2 million user comments per year (Häring, Loosen, & Maalej, 2018). Qualitative insights suggest that the image transfer from print to online was quite successful: SPON commenters expect other commenters on the site to be well educated, a promise for high-quality discussions. SPON users enjoy critical engagement with other users' comments—thus, the comment spaces on this outlet are considered the right place for those who like to engage others, in both playful and heated debate. An accompanying content analysis showed that the share of senior users, who had been active on the site for more than five years, was comparatively high. Accordingly, an engaged commenter described the community as "a little family." However, this "little family" can be perceived as not very open for those who cannot 'reach' the standard of argumentation set by skilled debaters, which is why some withdraw or do not even dare to engage in discussions on this platform (Springer, 2014).

Interaction patterns in communities also differ due to membership size, on which access requirements have considerable impact. A case study on HuffPost, for instance, showed how participation decreased when the news outlet shifted from anonymous and pseudonymous commenting to authentication via Facebook (Fredheim, Moore, & Naughton, 2015; see also Hille & Bakker, 2014). Higher participation hurdles are expected to discourage spammers, trolls, and opportunistic, spontaneous, less-committed "drive-by" commenters (Fredheim et al., 2015; Hille & Bakker, 2014). In addition, shifting user comments to social networking sites (SNSs) is likely to encourage interactivity (Wu & Atkin, 2017). While studies generally suggest that smaller groups with a limited number of members tend to exhibit stronger ties and higher interactivity, networked social structures with large and variable memberships tend to exhibit unbalanced and less-active communication between members, resulting in weaker ties and also higher likelihood of anti-social, stressful ties characterized by flaming, spamming and the like (Porter, 2004). In particular, organization-sponsored communities with a large membership, such as the commentary spaces on most news sites with a wider reach, will most likely exhibit attributes of both small groups and larger networks (ibid.). Accordingly, interactions between commenters on two larger German online news outlets' websites displayed more criticism than praise or support (Springer & Nuernbergk, 2016).

Unbalanced communication patterns in the form of "heavy," "moderate," and "light" commenting (Cho & Kwon, 2015, p. 369) have been well-documented (see also Figure 2.1). The predominant share of users are "light" commenters; in samples of content analyses from various cultural contexts, shares of one-timers' comments reach between 67% to over 80% (e.g., Graham & Wright, 2015; Ruiz et al., 2011; Springer, 2014). Commenters' communities, however, are certainly mainly driven by "moderate" and "heavy" users—who invest quite a bit of time and effort into this activity. As a result, users in these two groups often develop a sense of "ownership" over the comment spaces. Their activities are enabled and impacted by providers' infrastructures and modes of operation: (1) which articles they allow users to debate and which cannot be commented upon, (2) whether commenting requires registration or not, and (3) how commenting policies are defined and enforced through pre- and post-moderation (see Chapters 3 and 5). Since the news outlets are in control over these decisions, they impose additional, external, power structures on the users. Unsurprisingly, users can perceive registration requirements and applications of commenting policies as threats to free speech and the community management as a censoring bureau (Haim, Heinzel, Lankheit, Niagu, Springer, 2019; see also Häring et al., 2018; Robinson, 2010). It so happens that users experience the application of moderation rules resulting in non-publication or de-publication of their contributions as intransparent (Springer, 2014); especially so since the blocking of a comment is oftentimes only explained by a general statement with a reference to the commenting rules and therefore quite unspecific in the individual case. As established in Chapter 1, such rule-enforcing acts of moderation are usually not up for debate, thus commenters feel limited in their autonomy and freedom of speech. The experience of being powerless in the face of decisions they do not always understand can leave them frustrated and demotivated, with a feeling that the community management wanted to "crush" discussions with their actions (Springer, 2014; we discuss such de-motivations in the remainder of this chapter below). Current approaches in comment moderation that focus more on engagement with users and their contributions can thus be considered a step in the right direction (e.g., Haim et al., 2019). We discuss these ideas and practices in more depth in Chapter 5.

Profiling commenters and comment readers

The unbalanced communication patterns and the different channels news outlets use these days to reach their audiences make it challenging to determine who is actually a "news commenter" and who is part of such communities. Survey studies investigating the phenomenon of news commenting often ask for the frequency (e.g., "commented at least once," "at least once a month," or "at least once a week") and the channel (news outlets' websites, social media, or both). For instance, according to the latest representative and comparative figures from the Reuters Institute's "Digital News Report 2019," between 6% (Japan) and 45% (Turkey) of online users comment on news via social media or news outlets' websites in an average week (Newman Fletcher, Kalogeropoulos, & Kleis Nielsen, 2019). In most of the countries investigated, the rates reach between 12% (Denmark) and 29% (Poland, Portugal and the US). In Southeast Europe, shares between 31% and 45% are common (Greece: 31%, Romania: 32%, Bulgaria: 41%, Turkey: 45%), and the figures for Latin American countries are quite similar (Argentina: 31%, Brazil: 36%, Chile: 37%, Mexico: 43%).

A representative online survey in Germany conducted by Ziegele, Weber, and Köhler (as cited in Ziegele, Springer, Jost, & Wright, 2017, p. 324) differentiated between both channels and found that 23% of German online users commented on news outlets' websites at least once a month (12% at least once a week) and 25% commented on the Facebook pages of such outlets at least once a month (13% at least once a week). In regard to comment reading, 42% of German online users read comments on the news outlets' websites and 41% on the Facebook pages at least once a week. Thus, both channels seem to be equally popular. Concerning commenters' characteristics, the data also shows identical patterns for both channels: "lower education, frequent internet use, political interest, and a sympathy for the right-wing populist party 'Alternative für Deutschland' are the drivers of frequent comment-writing" (pp. 324–325).

Commenting on the news is a social phenomenon, and as such certainly subject to changes over time (Ziegele et al., 2017, pp. 326–327). This might explain the differences in commenters' sociodemographics, which emerge over the years of studying this phenomenon. Some examples for Germany: While Ziegele and colleagues found in their recent study that neither gender nor age significantly predicted commenting frequency (p. 325), earlier (but also non-representative) studies indicated that commenters were older than the average users of a news site (Ziegele et al., 2013; see also Springer et al., 2015). Men had also been previously found to be overrepresented among commenters (Köcher, 2016; Ziegele et al., 2013). While education turned out to be significantly negatively correlated with commenting frequency in the recent data, participants in the earlier survey mostly exhibited higher levels of education (Ziegele et al., 2013, pp. 88–91; see also Köcher, 2016).

Comparative data in regard to commenters' sociodemographics and traits are highly valuable, since it is very plausible that commenting on news might be quite a culture-specific activity: "[D]ifferent understandings of freedom of speech, different journalistic cultures, or varying degrees of technological affinity, and privacy concerns among internet users will result in different community structures or comment qualities" (Ziegele et al., 2017, p. 320). Hence, studies report some divergent findings throughout countries: While age was not found to be a significant predictor for commenting frequency in the latest German figures, it was negatively correlated with commenting frequency in a US survey (Meyer & Carey, 2014, p. 222; see also Stroud, Van Duyn, & Peacock, 2016). Similarly, commenting was found to be rather popular among younger users in Sweden (Bergström, 2008, p. 72). As for gender, the latest German figures deviate from available data in various cultural contexts suggesting men comment more frequently than women (e.g., Chung & Yoo, 2008; Friemel & Dötsch, 2015; Stroud et al., 2016). Delving deeper into these gender differences, Van Duyn, Peacock and Stroud (2019) show that women and men comment in different areas of a news site: "Men favor commenting on international, national, and state news at a consistently higher rate than do women. Alternatively, women report more commenting on local news articles than men do" (p. 10). A study in South Korea corroborated and extended these findings—differences in commenters' gender *and* age were found to vary across news topics (Lee & Ryu 2019): Sports, politics, technology, economy, and world news exhibited a clear domination of male commenters; the highest percentages of female commenters were found for the categories of "Entertainment/Celebrities," "Lifestyle," and "Crime & Accidents/Social Issues." Younger commenters tended to have more interest in "Entertainment/Celebrities" and sports, older commenters in politics and the economy (pp. 4–5, Tables 3 and 4).

However, other data reported above on predictors collected by Ziegele, Weber and Köhler (as cited in Ziegele et al., 2017) mostly conform with data that had been collected in other countries: Significant predictors for the usage of interactive features, such as the commentary feature, were found to be Internet efficacy/skill and interest in new technologies (Bergström, 2008; Chung & Yoo, 2008; Larsson, 2011), as well as political interest and engagement (Chung, 2008; Larsson, 2011).

Swiss data suggest that commenters are more conservative than comment readers (Friemel & Dötsch, 2015, p. 161), and comparative data reported in the Reuter's "Digital News Report 2019" suggest that people with populist attitudes are more likely to comment on news on social media, at least in Europe (Newman et al., 2019, p. 43). Similarly, another German study finds that commenters disproportionately support the right-wing populist party "Alternative for Germany" (AfD), the liberal party (FDP), and the "Pirate Party" (Köcher, 2016).

Comment readers, on the other hand, seem to be such a diverse group of users that a Swedish study could not find any characteristics concerning the socio-demography or traits of these so-called "lurkers," such as civic or political engagement (Larsson, 2011, p. 1190). However, they are very frequent and intense news site visitors (p. 1191). The aforementioned Swiss study suggests that, besides being more "left-leaning" than commenters, comment readers tend to be "younger than the average website user" (Friemel & Dötsch, 2015, p. 161). Hence, the authors assume that readers and writers of comments "differ significantly with respect to some central attributes" (p. 162). That both groups of users "are demographically distinct" is also highlighted by Stroud and colleagues (2016, p. 1) for the US: Compared to comment readers, American commenters "tend to be more male, have lower levels of education, and have lower incomes" (p. 5). Thus, it cannot be assumed that user commentary would provide its readers a "representative" reflection of opinion distributions, however, the function probably serves well to mobilize specific audience segments to make their thoughts public.

Motivations and inhibitors

Studies investigating why people comment on news or read the comments of others identified different factors that triggered commenting, but also sought to discover de-motivations that kept people from voicing their opinions. Since commenting starts—at least theoretically—with the article's input (see Figure 2.2), the topic should first of all influence the number of incoming comments as well as the manner in which people voice their opinions. Corroborating the finding that commenters are politically interested people (see passage above), available databases are solid enough to generalize that people all over the world love to discuss politics (e.g., Stroud et al., 2016; Ziegele et al., 2013, p. 89). This finding holds true in multi-country studies (Goodman, 2013), as well as studies of British (Richardson & Stanyer, 2011), German (Springer, 2014), Israeli (Tenenboim & Cohen, 2015),

Turkish (Ürper & Çevikel, 2014), and US (Boczkowski & Mitchelstein, 2012) news websites. Therefore, commentary spaces tend to become contested arenas for political discussions, which we discuss in more depth in Chapter 3. Richardson and Stanyer (2011) even showed that different media outlets relate to different commenting behaviors. On broadsheet sites, topics such as general domestic politics/party policies, US politics/elections, or foreign affairs attracted the most comments (p. 990), while on tabloid sites religion- and crime-related topics (p. 991) generated the most comments.

Not only the *article's topic* but also the *journalist and the journalistic contextualization and interpretations of events* influences the amount of incoming user feedback. Weber (2014), for instance, showed that the news factors proximity, impact, and frequency had a significant positive effect on the level of participation, while the news factor facticity had a negative one. If journalists describe an event factually, without providing further analysis or interpretation, the news story is less likely to attract commenters. If the journalistic contextualization or interpretation diverges from the perceptions and attitudes of the readers, this dissonance results in emotional pressure that some people try to ease by corrective commenting (Springer, 2014; see also Chung, Munno, & Moritz, 2015). The same holds true for "outraging posts" of fellow commenters (Springer, 2014). Some acts of news commenting can thus be conceptualized and understood as a media-/journalism-related form of civic engagement through which users try to impact the quality of the reporting—for instance, by giving their expertise or posting their (additional, divergent) viewpoints (ibid.; see also Stroud et al., 2016, p. 9).

Commenters' activity oscillates between one-time or rare usage and several thousand comments over the course of some years. Thus, it is analytically useful to distinguish between *entry motivations* and *motivations to remain* (Springer, 2014). The thrill of going public as well as the attempt to ease the pressure of cognitive dissonance that commenters experience while reading an article (user-content reaction; user-journalist interaction) or another user's comment (user-user interaction) were found to be relevant entry motivations (ibid.). Certainly, not only such "stimuli triggers" but also personality characteristics and situational conditions (for instance, life situations, daily routines, or even the time of day) impact which gratifications are sought through this online activity in a given moment or more generally over time (ibid.).

When asked about their motivation to engage, commenters mentioned or agreed (in varying degrees) to drivers that can be subsumed under the well-known categories "Uses-and-Gratification"-scholars established for traditional media usage. Summarized in all brevity: Besides a wish for *integration and social interaction*, which finds its expression in user-user and user-journalist interactivity (see Figure 2.2) and was already touched upon in the section on communities of commenters, users engage cognitively by *seeking or providing information/opinions* and *express and work on their personal identity*; that is, they use their arguments as a means of self-presentation, or expressions of others as a means for social comparison. Additionally, they comment for affective reasons—for their *entertainment and relaxation* (e.g., Chung & Yoo, 2008; Diakopoulos & Naaman, 2011; Springer, 2014; Springer et al., 2015; Wu & Atkin, 2017; Yoo, 2011). As discussed in the previous section, context factors such as the websites' design and the community that gathers around the outlet certainly also impact which gratifications are obtained and then sought after in future commenting (motivations to remain). A study on US-college students by Wu and Atkin (2017) also suggests that motivational drivers for commenting differ depending on the channel: "informing, [attention seeking] exhibitionism, and obtaining feedback are found predictive of the frequency of commenting on online news comment sections, while social connection turns out to be the only predictor of posting on SNSs" (p. 75). Similar differences were also reported for Argentinian users commenting on blogs versus posting comments to online newspaper sites (Mitchelstein, 2011): "commenting in newspapers is usually related to self-expression motives (make opinions public, let off steam), whereas participating in blogs is mostly linked to communication with others (discuss issues, meet people) and entertainment motives (fun)" (p. 2021).

Drivers to comment thus oscillate between desires related to self (that is, internal psychological processes) and desires related to others or, more generally, users' integration into a community and eventually, into society. It is even obvious that "self" doesn't go without others: The social setting in which commenting is embedded provides the input for self-evaluation processes and entertaining experiences, and serves to gratify a need for attention and recognition (e.g., Barnes, 2015, p. 822; Springer, 2014; Wu & Atkin, 2017, p. 74). Yet data also suggest that commenters who score higher on the social-integrative dimension cannot always satisfy their need to socialize to the desired extent through the use of interactive features and become frustrated over time (Springer, 2014; Springer et al., 2015; Yoo, 2011). This could be caused by the fact that discussion with others always implies the persuasion of dissenters, and that understanding is complicated due to the fact that commenters are often opinionated and thus quite resistant (e.g., Springer, 2014; Springer et al., 2015; see also Stroud et al., 2016, p. 12). That worldviews are usually not given up so easily probably also explains why US commenters, when asked if they avoided commenting on particular news topics, most often said they stay away from "religion and spirituality" as well as "U.S. politics or domestic policy" (Stroud et al., 2016, p. 11). Discussions on these topics also tend to become uncivil and thus disengaging. Furthermore, social-interactive motivations were found to not only be directed at users, but also at journalists (e.g., Heise, Loosen, Reimer, & Schmidt, 2014, p. 418; Springer, 2014; Springer et al., 2015). However, the regular absence of the authors in user discussions below their articles (Graham & Wright, 2015; Jakobs, 2014, p. 201; Ksiazek, 2018a; Singer, 2009; Wolfgang, 2018) can be frustrating for users seeking to reach journalists or getting their attention publicly (Robinson, 2010, p. 137; Springer, 2014). Moreover, intransparent and overprotective, but also absent moderation was found to evoke dissatisfaction (Springer, 2014; see also Robinson, 2010).

Beyond the analysis of such de-motivations, studies also investigated why some people would not want to voice their opinions publicly. Besides restrictive time budgets (e.g., Barnes, 2015), people are hesitant to register and concerned about data protection (Springer et al., 2015). Another reason is simply the lack of personal involvement (Springer, 2014; Ziegele, 2016). A low sense of opinionation can be caused by disinterest, but comment readers of an Australian alternative journalism website also expressed intimidation by the "textual authority portrayed by other commenters or the journalist" (Barnes, 2015, p. 817), indicating low levels of confidence (p. 818) and the subjective perception of lacking competence (see also Springer, 2014; Stroud et al., 2016).

Furthermore, the perceived "quality" of discussions was found to hamper not only participation, but also reader interest (Springer, 2014; Springer et al., 2015). For instance, Diakopoulos and Naaman (2011, p. 136; see also Stroud et al., 2016, p. 13) show that non-users would not read comments on a Californian news site because they think that comments are off-topic, too argumentative, and uncivil. Problematic commenting behaviors were found to be more prevalent in specific areas (see Chapter 3), which is probably why "religion and spirituality" ranked highest among topics that US comment readers said they would avoid (Stroud et al., 2016, p. 12). It is reasonable to assume that people do not want to learn about opinions of mean-spirited individuals. Nevertheless, studies worldwide suggest that a fair share of news audiences see comments as an "integral part of the overall story"

(Barnes, 2015, p. 820; see also Bergström & Wadbring, 2015, p. 147). This is certainly because a broad variety of the motivations that were found to trigger active commenting drive comment reading as well (e.g., Diakopoulos & Naaman, 2011; Stroud et al., 2016): Commenting features provide access to other peoples' opinions and can thus gratify especially information-related and society-monitoring needs but also identity-related needs such as social comparison. Moreover, reading comments can also be quite entertaining—for instance, to observe and follow a heated public dispute (Springer, 2014).

In summary, the research literature suggests that commenting on the news is an activity that engages some users to varying degrees, but certainly not all users. Less engaged, committed commenters will walk away when the initial excitement wears off and recognition, stimulating interaction, and persuasion fail to materialize. Continuous commenting will be fueled by a sustained enjoyment of cognitive, social-integrative, identity-related, and affective gratifications. Especially interesting for scholarly work are those users that are driven to critically engage with media coverage and other users, by contributing their opinions in polarized societal debates (as acts of deliberation; see Chapter 3). These are the motivations of users for whom the comment features had been designed and installed in the first place. However, the nature of comment threads (e.g., that user discussions usually 'head nowhere') and the way some users take advantage of the commenting feature (e.g., to vent and communicate anti-socially) can start to frustrate and crowd out even the most committed users. We suggest that these two aspects should be focal points for media organizations that endeavor to save the comment spaces, if an abandonment of these public places for debate is not in their interest. In particular, experimentation with automated processing of user comments is especially promising. We delve deeper into this in Chapter 5.

References

Anderson, C. W. (2011). Between creative and quantified audiences: Web metrics and changing patterns of newswork in local US newsrooms. *Journalism, 12*(5), 550–566. doi: 10.1177/1464884911402451

Arenberg, T., & Lowrey, W. (2019). The impact of web metrics on community news decisions: A resource dependence perspective. *Journalism & Mass Communication Quarterly, 96*(1), 131–149. doi: 10.1177/1077699018801318

Barnes, R. (2015). Understanding the affective investment produced through commenting on Australian alternative journalism website New Matilda. *New Media & Society, 17*(5), 810–826. doi: 10.1177/1461444813511039

Beckett, L. (2010). Getting beyond just pageviews: Philly.com's seven-part equation for measuring online engagement. *Nieman Reports*. Retrieved from: http://www.niemanlab.org/2010/10/getting-beyond-just-pageviews-philly-coms-seven-part-equation-for-measuring-online-engagement/

Bergström, A. (2008). The reluctant audience: Online participation in the Swedish journalistic context. *Westminster Papers in Communication & Culture, 5*(2), 60–79. doi: 10.16997/wpcc.67

Bergström, A., & Wadbring, I. (2015). Beneficial yet crappy: Journalists and audiences on obstacles and opportunities in reader comments. *European Journal of Communication, 30*(2), 137–151. doi: 10.1177/0267323114559378

Boczkowski, P. J., & Mitchelstein, E. (2012). How users take advantage of different forms of interactivity on online news sites: Clicking, e-mailing, and commenting. *Human Communication Research, 38*(1), 1–22. doi: 10.1111/j.1468-2958.2011.01418.x

Brodie, R. J., Ilic, A., Juric, B., & Hollebeek, L. (2013). Consumer engagement in a virtual brand community: An exploratory analysis. *Journal of Business Research, 66*, 105–114. doi: 10.1016/j.jbusres.2011.07.029

Canter, L. (2013). The misconception of online comment threads: Content and control on local newspaper websites. *Journalism Practice, 7*(5), 604–619. doi: 10.1080/17512786.2012.740172

Cho, D., & Kwon, K. H. (2015). The impacts of identity verification and disclosure of social cues on flaming in online user comments. *Computers in Human Behavior, 51*, 363–372. doi: 10.1016/j.chb.2015.04.046

Chung, D. S. (2008). Interactive features of online newspapers: Identifying patterns and predicting use of engaged readers. *Journal of Computer-Mediated Communication, 13*(3), 658–679. doi: 10.1111/j.1083-6101.2008.00414.x

Chung, D. S., & Yoo, C. Y. (2008). Audience motivations for using interactive features: Distinguishing use of different types of interactivity on an online newspaper. *Mass Communication and Society, 11*(4), 375–397. doi: 10.1080/15205430701791048

Chung, M., Munno, G. J., & Moritz, B. (2015). Triggering participation: Exploring the effects of third-person and hostile media perceptions on online participation. *Computers in Human Behavior, 53*, 452–461. doi: 10.1016/j.chb.2015.06.037

Diakopoulos, N., & Naaman, M. (2011). Towards quality discourse in online news comments. *Proceedings of CSCW 2011* (pp. 133–142). March 19–23, Hangzhou, China. doi: 10.1145/1958824.1958844

Esau, K., Friess, D., & Eilders, C. (2017). Design matters! An empirical analysis of online deliberation on different news platforms. *Policy & Internet, 9*(3), 321–342. doi: 10.1002/poi3.154

Ferrucci, P. (2018). It is in the numbers: How market orientation impacts journalists' use of news metrics. *Journalism*. Advance Online Publication. doi: 10.1177/1464884918807056

Fredheim, R., Moore, A., & Naughton, J. (2015). Anonymity and online commenting: The broken windows effect and the end of drive-by commenting.

Proceedings of the ACM Web Science Conference. June 28–July 1, Oxford, UK. doi: 10.1145/2786451.2786459

Friemel, T. N., & Dötsch, M. (2015). Online reader comments as indicator for perceived public opinion. In M. Emmer, & C. Strippel (Eds.), *Kommunikationspolitik für die digitale Gesellschaft* (pp. 151–172). doi: 10.17174/dcr.v1.8

Goodman, E. (2013). Online comment moderation: Emerging best practices. *World Association of Newspapers (WAN-IFRA)*. Retrieved from http://www.wan-ifra.org/reports/2013/10/04/online-comment-moderation-emerging-best-practices

Graham, T., & Wright, S. (2015). A tale of two stories from “Below the Line” comment fields at the Guardian. *The International Journal of Press/Politics, 20*(3), 317–338. doi: 10.1177/1940161215581926

Haim, M., Heinzel, I., Lankheit, S., Niagu, A. M., & Springer, N. (2019, May). *Identifying the good and the bad: Using machine learning to moderate user commentary on news*. Paper presentation at the annual International Communication Association (ICA) conference, Washington, DC.

Hanusch, F., & Tandoc Jr., E. C. (2019). Comments, analytics, and social media: The impact of audience feedback on journalists' market orientation. *Journalism, 20*(6), 695–713. doi: 10.1177/1464884917720305

Häring, M., Loosen, W., & Maalej, W. (2018). Who is addressed in this comment? Automatically classifying meta-comments in news comments. *Proceedings of the ACM on Human-Computer Interaction*. November 3–7, New York. doi: 10.1145/3274336

Heise, N., Loosen, W., Reimer, J., & Schmidt, J. H. (2014). Including the audience: Comparing the attitudes and expectations of journalists and users towards participation in German TV news journalism. *Journalism Studies, 15*(4), 411–430. doi: 10.1080/1461670X.2013.831232

Hermida, A. (2011a). Mechanisms of participation: How audience options shape the conversation. In J. B. Singer, A. Hermida, D. Domingo, A. Heinonen, S. Paulussen, T. Quandt, … (Eds.), *Participatory journalism. Guarding open gates at online newspapers* (pp. 13–33). Sussex: Wiley-Blackwell.

Hille, S., & Bakker, P. (2014). Engaging the social news user. Comments on news sites and Facebook. *Journalism Practice, 8*(5), 563–572. doi: 10.1080/17512786.2014.899758

Hollebeek, L. D. (2011). Demystifying customer brand engagement: Exploring the loyalty nexus. *Journal of Marketing Management, 27*(7–8), 785–807. doi: 10.1080/0267257X.2010.500132

Hollebeek, L. D., Glynn, M. S., & Brodie, R. J. (2014). Consumer brand engagement in social media: Conceptualization, scale development and validation. *Journal of Interactive Marketing, 28*, 149–165. doi: 10.1016/j.intmar.2013.12.002

IAB. (2014). Defining and measuring digital ad engagement in a cross-platform world. *Interactive Advertising Bureau*. Retrieved from http://www.iab.net/media/file/Ad_Engagement_Spectrum2014_FINAL2-5-2014-EB.PDF

Jakobs, I. (2014). Diskutieren für mehr Demokratie? Zum deliberativen Potenzial von Leserkommentaren zu journalistischen Texten im Internet. In W. Loosen, & M. Dohle (Eds.), *Journalismus und (sein) Publikum* (pp. 191–210). Wiesbaden: Springer.

Köcher, R. (2016). Flüchtlingszustrom: Auswirkungen eines gesellschaftlichen Aufregungszyklus auf politisches Interesse und Mediennutzung. *AWA 2016*. Retrieved from http://www.ifd-allensbach.de/fileadmin/AWA/AWA_Praesentationen/2016/AWA_2016_Koecher_Fluechtlingskrise_Medien.pdf

Ksiazek, T. B. (2018a). Commenting on the news: Explaining the degree and quality of user comments on news websites. *Journalism Studies, 19*(5), 650–673. doi: 10.1080/1461670X.2016.1209977

Ksiazek, T. B. (2018b). Ratings analysis. In P. Napoli (Ed.), *Mediated communication. Handbooks of communication science series* (pp. 213–224). Berlin, Boston: de Gruyter Mouton.

Ksiazek, T. B., Peer, L., & Lessard, K. (2014). User engagement with online news: Conceptualizing interactivity and exploring the relationship between online news videos and user comments. *New Media & Society, 18*(3), 502–520. doi: 10.1177/1461444814545073

Larsson, A. O. (2011). Interactive to me – interactive to you? A study of use and appreciation of interactivity on Swedish newspaper websites. *New Media & Society, 13*(7), 1180–1197. doi: 10.1177/1461444811401254

Lee, S. Y., & Ryu, M. H. (2019). Exploring characteristics of online news comments and commenters with machine learning approaches. *Telematics and Informatics, 43*. doi: 10.1016/j.tele.2019.101249

Lewis, S. C., Holton, A. E., & Coddington, M. (2014). Reciprocal journalism. *Journalism Practice, 8*(2), 229–241. doi: 10.1080/17512786.2013.85984

Lowrey, W., & Woo, C. W. (2010). The news organization in uncertain times: Business or institution? *Journalism & Mass Communication Quarterly, 87*(1), 41–61. doi: 10.1177/107769901008700103

Malthouse, E. C., Haenlein, M., Skiera, B., Wege, E., & Zhang, M. (2013). Managing customer relationships in the social media era: Introducing the social CRM house. *Journal of Interactive Marketing, 27*, 270–280. doi: 10.1016/j.intmar.2013.9.008

McMillan, D. W., & Chavis, D. M. (1986). Sense of community: A definition and theory. *Journal of Community Psychology, 14*(1), 6–23. doi: 10.1002/1520-6629(198601)14:1<6::AID-JCOP2290140103>3.0.CO;2-I

Meyer, H. K., & Carey, M. C. (2014). In moderation: Examining how journalists' attitudes toward online comments affect the creation of community. *Journalism Practice, 8*(2), 213–228. doi: 10.1080/17512786.2013.859838

Mitchelstein, E. (2011). Catharsis and community: Divergent motivations for audience participation in online newspapers and blogs. *International Journal of Communication, 5*, 2014–2034. Retrieved from https://ijoc.org/index.php/ijoc/article/view/1080

Napoli, P. (2011). *Audience evolution: New technologies and the transformation of media audiences*. New York: Columbia University Press.

Nelson, J. L. (2019). The next media regime: The pursuit of 'audience engagement' in journalism. *Journalism*. Advance Online Publication. doi: 10.1177/1464884919862375

Newman, N., Fletcher, R., Kalogeropoulos, A., & Kleis Nielsen, R. (2019). Reuters Institute Digital News Report 2019. *Reuters Institute for the Study of Journalism*. Retrieved from https://reutersinstitute.politics.ox.ac.uk/sites/default/files/inline-files/DNR_2019_FINAL.pdf

Peterson, E. T., & Carabis, J. (2008). Measuring the immeasurable: Visitor engagement. *Web Analytics Demystified*. Retrieved from http://www.webanalyticsdemystified.com/downloads/Web_Analytics_Demystified_and_NextStage_Global_-_Measuring_the_Immeasurable_-_Visitor_Engagement.pdf

Petre, C. (2015). The traffic factories: Metrics at Chartbeat, Gawker Media, and The New York Times. *Tow Center for Digital Journalism*. Retrieved from http://towcenter.org/research/traffic-factories/

Picone, I., Kleut, J., Pavlíčková, T., Romic, B., Møller Hartley, J., & De Ridder, S. (2019). Small acts of engagement: Reconnecting productive audience practices with everyday agency. *New Media & Society, 21*(9), 2010–2028. doi: 10.1177/1461444819837569

Porter, C. E. (2004). A typology of virtual communities: A multi-disciplinary foundation for future research. *Journal of Computer-Mediated Communication, 10*(1). doi: 10.1111/j.1083-6101.2004.tb00228.x

Reader, B. (2015). *Audience feedback in the news media*. New York: Routledge.

Richardson, J. E., & Stanyer, J. (2011). Reader opinion in the digital age: Tabloid and broadsheet newspaper websites and the exercise of political voice. *Journalism, 12*(8), 983–1003. doi: 10.1177/1464884911415974

Robinson, S. (2010). Traditionalists vs. convergers: Textual privilege, boundary work, and the journalist—Audience relationship in the commenting policies of online news sites. *Convergence: The International Journal of Research into New Media Technologies, 16*(1), 125–143. doi: 10.1177/1354856509347719

Ruiz, C., Domingo, D., Micó, J. L., Díaz-Noci, J., Meso, K., & Masip, P. (2011). Public sphere 2.0? The democratic qualities of citizen debates in online newspapers. *The International Journal of Press/Politics, 16*(4), 463–487. doi: 10.1177/1940161211415849

Singer, J. B. (2009). Separate spaces: Discourse about the 2007 Scottish elections on a national newspaper web site. *The International Journal of Press/Politics, 14*(4), 477–496. doi: 10.1177/1940161209336659

Singer, J. B., Hermida, A., Domingo, D., Heinonen, A., Paulussen, S., Quandt, T., …, Vujnovic, M. (Eds.). (2011). *Participatory journalism. Guarding open gates at online newspapers*. Sussex: Wiley-Blackwell.

Slavtcheva-Petkova, V. (2016). Are newspapers' online discussion boards democratic tools or conspiracy theories' engines? A case study on an Eastern European "media war." *Journalism & Mass Communication Quarterly, 93*(4), 1115–1134. doi: 10.1177/1077699015610880

Spiegel (n.d.). "Sturmgeschütz der Demokratie." *Spiegel Online*. Retrieved from https://www.spiegel.de/politik/deutschland/die-geschichte-der-spiegel-gruppe-sturmgeschuetz-der-demokratie-a-221730.html

Springer, N. (2014). *Beschmutzte Öffentlichkeit? Warum Menschen die Kommentarfunktion auf Online-Nachrichtenseiten als öffentliche Toilettenwand benutzen, warum Besucher ihre Hinterlassenschaften trotzdem lesen, und wie die Wände im Anschluss aussehen*. Berlin: LIT Verlag Münster.

Springer, N., Engelmann, I., & Pfaffinger, C. (2015). User comments: Motives and inhibitors to write and read. *Information, Communication & Society. 18*(7), 798–815. doi: 10.1080/1369118X.2014.997268

Springer, N., & Nuernbergk, C. (2016, June). *Commenting user networks: Two case studies on interactions and behavioral self-regulation in comments sections*. Paper presentation at the annual International Communication Association (ICA) conference, Fukuoka, Japan.

Stroud, N. J., Van Duyn, E., & Peacock, C. (2016). News commenters and news comment readers. *Engaging News Project. Annette Strauss Institute for Civic Life*, University of Texas at Austin. Retrieved from https://mediaengagement.org/wp-content/uploads/2016/03/ENP-News-Commenters-and-Comment-Readers1.pdf

Taddicken, M., & Bund, K. (2010). Ich kommentiere, also bin ich. Community Research am Beispiel des Diskussionsforums der Zeit Online. In M. Welker, & C. Wünsch (Eds.), *Die Online-Inhaltsanalyse. Forschungsobjekt Internet* (pp. 167–190). Köln: von Halem.

Tenenboim, O., & Cohen, A. A. (2015). What prompts users to click and comment: A longitudinal study of online news. *Journalism, 16*(2), 198–217. doi: 10.1177/1464884913513996

Ürper, D. Ç., & Çevikel, T. (2014). Reader comments on mainstream online newspapers in Turkey: Perceptions of web editors and moderators. *Communications, 39*(4), 483–503. doi: 10.1515/commun-2014-0022

Van Duyn, E., Peacock, C., & Stroud, N. J. (2019). The gender gap in online news comment sections. *Social Science Computer Review*. Advance Online Publication. doi: 10.1177/0894439319864876

Vivek, S. D., Beatty, S. E., & Morgan, R. M. (2012). Customer engagement: Exploring customer relationships beyond purchase. *Journal of Marketing Theory and Practice, 20*(2), 127–145. doi: 10.2753/MTP1069-6679200201

Watson, B. R., Peng, Z., & Lewis, S. C. (2019). Who will intervene to save news comments? Deviance and social control in communities of news commenters. *New Media & Society*. Advance Online Publication. doi: 1461444819828328

Weber, P. (2014). Discussions in the comments section: Factors influencing participation and interactivity in online newspapers' reader comments. *New Media & Society, 16*(6), 941–957. doi: 10.1177/1461444813495165

Wiesenfeld, E. (1996). The concept of "we": A community social psychology myth? *Journal of Community Psychology, 24*(4), 337–346. doi: 10.1002/(SICI)1520-6629(199610)24:4<337::AID-JCOP4>3.0.CO;2-R

Wolfgang, J. D. (2018). Cleaning up the "fetid swamp:" Examining how journalists construct policies and practices for moderating comments. *Digital Journalism, 6*(1), 21–40. doi: 10.1080/21670811.2017.1343090

Wu, T. Y., & Atkin, D. (2017). Online news discussions: Exploring the role of user personality and motivations for posting comments on news. *Journalism & Mass Communication Quarterly, 94*(1), 61–80. doi: 10.1177/1077699016655754

Yoo, C. Y. (2011). Modeling audience interactivity as the gratification-seeking process in online newspapers. *Communication Theory, 21*(1), 67–89. doi: 10.1111/j.1468-2885.2010.01376.x

Ziegele, M. (2016). *Nutzerkommentare als Anschlusskommunikation. Theorie und qualitative Analyse des Diskussionswerts von Online-Nachrichten.* Wiesbaden: VS.

Ziegele, M., Breiner, T., & Quiring O. (2014). What creates interactivity in online news discussions? An exploratory analysis of discussion factors in user comments on news items. *Journal of Communication, 64*(6), 1111–1138. doi: 10.1111/jcom.12123

Ziegele, M., Johnen, M., Bickler, A., Jakobs, I., Setzer, T., & Schnauber, A. (2013). Männlich, rüstig, kommentiert? Einflussfaktoren auf die Aktivität kommentierender Nutzer von Online-Nachrichtenseiten. *Studies in Communication and Media, 3*(1), 67–114. doi: 10.5771/2192-4007-2013-1-67

Ziegele, M., Springer, N., Jost, P., & Wright, S. (2017). Online user comments across news and other content formats: multidisciplinary perspectives, new directions. *Studies in Communication and Media, 6*(4), 315–332. doi: 10.5771/2192-4007-2017-4-315

3 Comments as public engagement

Building on our conceptual model of user engagement and the Thread Structure Model in the preceding chapter, deliberation is a particular manifestation of commenting that signifies high-level cognitive/emotional investment on the part of users. User contributions to the deliberative qualities of a particular commenting forum can come in the form of user-content reactions (e.g., posting a comment in response to the article to share an opinion or perspective on a news topic), user-user interactions (both discussion and dialogue), and user-journalist interactions.

In this chapter, we discuss user commentary as a form of *public* engagement, drawing on the philosophical foundations of the public sphere within deliberative democracies. We then move to an in-depth treatment of (in)civility in user comments, integrating our theoretical and empirical work. Next, we offer a discussion of viewpoint diversity and commenting effects in the context of commentary as public engagement. Since deliberation can, of course, only explain some forms of user commentary, we conclude by offering alternative commentary frameworks beyond a traditional deliberation model.

Public sphere and deliberative democracy

Research on user comments traditionally draws on philosophical notions of the public sphere as an overarching theoretical framework. This understanding of comments adapts the work of Habermas (1989) to describe a space where the public can engage in rational, civil discussion about the important events and issues of the day. Unlike the in-person coffee houses and salons that Habermas depicted, comments are seen as a *virtual* opportunity for engaging in public deliberation.

There is no doubt that digital technologies afford the opportunity for public engagement with and deliberation about current events, and most scholars point to news websites—and stories about politics in particular (e.g., Boczkowski & Mitchelstein, 2012; Díaz Noci, Domingo, Masip, Lluís Micó, & Ruiz, 2010; Richardson & Stanyer, 2011; Ruiz et al., 2011)—as the place where these socially and politically significant discussions are most likely to manifest. Yet whether these spaces have realized the potential to facilitate healthy deliberation rests on the degree to which these virtual discussions can be characterized as civil. While there is a growing body of literature addressing this question, the research on civility and hostility in online deliberation is decidedly mixed.

(In)civility in user comments

While both journalists and users see the deliberative potential in commenting platforms, there is widespread concern about the quality of discussion occurring in these spaces (Barnes, 2015; Goodman, 2013; Lee, 2012; Meltzer, 2015; Nielsen, 2012; Santana, 2011, 2014; Springer, Engelmann, & Pfaffinger, 2015). A 2013 study from The World Association of Newspapers conducted interviews with news professionals from over 100 organizations across 63 countries, and found that journalists valued user comments, particularly for engaging users, promoting loyalty, and encouraging community, but they also expressed concern about the general quality of these discussions and the resources necessary to curate productive discussion spaces (Goodman, 2013). Similarly, Meltzer (2015) analyzed industry discourse about user comments, finding widespread concern among news professionals about incivility in comments.

That sentiment was echoed in our analysis of recent public statements from news organizations about their rationale for removing the option to comment. We found extensive references to incivility as a reason for removing commentary functions. The specific language we identified pointed to concerns about prejudicial statements, misogyny, racism, and more general abuse—all of which would be more generally characterized as incivility. Others have found similar evidence that journalists and news organizations see a need to improve the quality of user comments (e.g., Nielsen, 2012; Santana, 2011) and that journalists and their organizations should be responsible for encouraging more civil discussion. In response to these concerns, we have seen the emergence of a substantial body of research on the quality of user comments, focusing particularly on the civil and/or hostile nature of user comments.

Approaches to studying (in)civility in user comments are varied. Some studies analyze the degree of civility in online discussion (e.g., Benson, 1996; Díaz Noci et al., 2010; Ng & Detenber, 2005; Papacharissi, 2004; Richardson & Stanyer, 2011; Ruiz et al., 2011; Zhou, Chan, & Peng, 2008), while others focus specifically on hostility (e.g., Alonzo & Aiken, 2004; Lee, 2005; Moor, Heuvelman, & Verleur, 2010; O'Sullivan & Flanagin, 2003). While these would seem to coexist (i.e., it is possible that a particular discussion can exhibit both civil and hostile qualities), many studies restrict their focus to one or the other.

Conceptualizations of civility and hostility vary from normative to contextual definitions (Ksiazek, Peer, & Zivic, 2015). Normative understandings emphasize broadly applicable definitions, and typically identify hostility with qualities like hate speech, profanity, and obscene or offensive language, while civility is generally understood as the absence of these qualities (Alonzo & Aiken, 2004; Ferree, Gamson, Gerhards, & Rucht, 2002; Lee, 2005; Moor et al., 2010; Ng & Detenber, 2005; Zhou et al., 2008). Contextual definitions emphasize the socially constructed, emergent nature of online discussion and argue for contextually situated understandings of civility and hostility (Himelboim, 2011; Hurrell, 2005; Neurauter-Kessels, 2011; O'Sullivan & Flanagin, 2003; Papacharissi, 2004). These contextual understandings foreground the shared values and norms of particular virtual communities in which commentary takes place (see Chapter 2).

Hostility, or incivility, is commonly identified as comments "intentionally designed to attack someone or something and, in doing so, incite anger or exasperation through the use of name-calling, character assassination, offensive language, profanity, and/or insulting language" (Ksiazek et al., 2015, p. 854). Civility is less easily defined. While Herbst (2010, p. 19) offers a useful conceptualization of civility as "constructive engagement with others through argument, deliberation, and discourse," Ksiazek and colleagues (2015) find that much of the literature simply treats civility as the absence of hostility. Ksiazek and Peer (2016) identify a broadly applicable conceptual definition of a civil comment as one that "moves a discussion forward without name-calling, stereotyping, or being written solely to incite anger from another side of the argument" (p. 245). In other words, it is a comment meant to contribute to a user discussion that is absent of hostility.

Coming to conceptual terms with civility has been difficult (Jamieson, Volinsky, Weitz, & Kenski, 2017), as some scholars define civility in broad, normative terms, while others treat it as a phenomenon that is socially constructed and contextually situated (Herbst, 2010). Normative definitions situate civility in the context of generally held standards for civil discourse. Here, civility is typically identified by the avoidance of personal attacks and harsh language used against other users/journalists (user-user and user-journalist interaction) or the content being discussed (user-content reaction) (Zhou et al., 2008).

Much of what we see in normative definitions of civility seems to require users to engage in polite interaction. For instance, Ng and

Detenber (2005) equated civility with politeness and considered any "rude comments, name-calling, and personal attacks" to be examples of incivility (p. 8). However, others disagree with this general approach, arguing that civility and politeness are not the same thing (Papacharissi, 2004; Reader, 2012; Schudson, 1997; Sifianou, 2019). For instance, Schudson (1997) suggests that democratic dialogue might be stifled if people are too concerned with being civil, and healthy deliberation sometimes needs to be robust and impolite. Similarly, Papacharissi (2004) argued, "It is not civility that limits the democratic potential of conversation, but rather, a confusion of politeness with civility. It is adherence to etiquette that frequently restricts conversation, by making it reserved, tepid, less spontaneous" (p. 260). In other words, robust deliberation could include impolite behavior and still be considered civil. Herbst (2010) argues for a "culture of argument," where civility is preferred, but incivility can also productively contribute to user discussions. In fact, Coe, Kenski and Rains (2014) found that uncivil comments were more likely to include evidence than civil comments, concluding, "Contrary to the idea that incivility and poor argumentation go hand in hand, use of evidence and incivility were actually a more common pairing than were a lack of evidence and incivility" (p. 673).

In contrast to normative conceptualizations, some favor a more contextual understanding of civility, highlighting the unique, socially constructed nature of what civility means for a given discussion group. For instance, Papacharissi (2004) conceptualized civility as behavior that is not offensive to the social group(s) in which the behavior exists. Similarly, Hurrell (2005) argued that civility is discursively constructed within each community and common notions of civility can privilege certain types of people depending on their class, race/ethnicity, or educational background.

Much like the civility literature, the scholarship on hostility, or incivility, also wrestles with normative versus contextual definitions. Research on hostility is generally divided across studies of general aggression/antagonism, flaming (which includes aggression/antagonism, but also swearing, hate speech, and a wealth of other indicators of hostility), and trolling (see Hardaker (2010) for a review of varied conceptualizations). Normative conceptualizations define hostility as comments that are profane, insulting, obscene, or otherwise offensive (Alonzo & Aiken, 2004; Lee, 2005; Moor et al., 2010). In our analysis of commentary removal statements, we found extensive references to normative concerns about incivility (see Chapter 6). Alternatively, contextual understandings of hostility highlight the set of interactional norms for the group in which a message exists (Neurauter-Kessels, 2011; O'Sullivan & Flanagin, 2003). Once again, we see contrasting schools of thought: one focusing on broadly applicable, normative definitions; the other arguing that hostility is emergent and socially constructed in unique contexts that are particular to a given thread structure.

Research suggests that (in)civility in comments can be explained by a variety of factors, including: story topic, use of sources in an article, journalist participation in comment threads, and organizational commenting policies (See Table 3.1). Much of the empirical research presented below (including Table 3.1) and in Chapters 4 and 5 comes

Table 3.1 Predictors of user engagement (number of comments) and civility/hostility in comments

	More	*Less*

Number of comments	• Controversial story topics (e.g., gun control)
	• Multimedia features
	• Journalist participation
	• Commenting policies
	  • User registration
	    • on-site (pseudonymous)
	    • third-party (publicly identifiable social cues)
	  • Post-moderation
	  • Reputation management
	  • Private messaging
		• Commenting policies
		  • Pre-moderation
		  • Prohibiting anonymity

Civility	• Commenting policies
	  • Pre-moderation
	  • Post-moderation
	  • Reputation management
		• Story topics
		  • Economy
		  • Government inefficiency
		• Commenting policies
		  • Prohibiting anonymity

Hostility	• Story topics
	  • Gun control
	  • Foreign policy
	  • Intelligence agencies
	• Use of sources in an article
	• Commenting policies
	  • Private messaging
		• Story topics
		  • Labor
		• Journalist participation
		• Commenting policies
		  • User registration
		    • third-party (publicly identifiable social cues)
		  • Pre-moderation
		  • Prohibiting anonymity

Summary of results from Ksiazek's (2015, 2018) analysis of 333,605 user comments across 1,379 news stories from 20 US/UK news websites.

from a study conducted by Ksiazek (2015, 2018). As such, it is worth offering some explanation about the research method used in that study (see Ksiazek (2015, 2018) for a full, detailed description).

The sample was drawn from a seven-day composite week in 2013 across 20 US/UK news websites, resulting in 1,379 stories, 333,605 comments, and 14,497,029 words of comment text. On the selected days, custom software crawled the top online news sites in the United States ranked by Average Monthly Unique Visitors. Stories were collected from the political news pages of the following news websites: Yahoo! News, CNN, MSNBC, New York Times, ABC News, Huffington Post, Washington Post, CBS News, USA Today, LA Times, NY Daily News, BBC, Examiner, Slate, Topix, Boston.com, Guardian, NPR, Chicago Tribune, and Wall Street Journal. The selection of sites includes a mix of organizations whose primary business resides in print, TV, radio, and online, meeting a growing call for studies of media use that integrate multiple platforms (e.g., Taneja, Webster, Malthouse, & Ksiazek, 2012). The list of sites also includes regional, national, and international (US/UK) news outlets, as well as both traditional and digital-native news outlets. The custom data collection program archived all political news stories from each site on the selected days, as well as all comments posted to each story.

The dependent variables (number of comments, civility, hostility) were captured through automated content analytic procedures. The number of comments posted to each story was publicly available and the custom crawler program captured this measure during the initial phase of data collection. To assess civility and hostility in user comments, custom dictionaries were developed by integrating operational definitions from the literature (e.g., Alonzo & Aiken, 2004; Lee, 2005; Ng & Detenber, 2005; Turnage, 2007), existing word dictionaries from the widely used text mining program Linguistic Inquiry and Word Count, or LIWC (Pennebaker, Booth, & Francis, 2007), and a qualitative analysis to account for any additional civil and hostile terms that may be unique to the users who comment on political news stories. The custom civility dictionary combined LIWC's dictionaries of positive emotion, assent and insight words (e.g., "agreement," "consider," "respect"). The custom hostility dictionary combined dictionaries of negative emotion, anger and swear words (e.g., "coward," "hate," "kill"). Terms from the qualitative analysis were added to the custom dictionaries. For instance, in the context of political news, words like "illegals" or "aliens" were often used in hostile comments about immigration policies. The final dictionaries include 621 civil words and 399 hostile words.

The custom dictionaries were then implemented in LIWC to create separate numerical indices of civility and hostility for the set of comments posted to each story. The measures capture the number of civil or hostile words, respectively, as a percentage of total words for a given set of comments. For instance, if LIWC identifies five hostile words in a set of comments containing 100 words, then the hostility score is 5% for that story. These proportional measures control for the number of comments so that a story with 30 comments can have the same hostility score as one with 3,000 comments.

Subsequently, two research assistants hand-coded each story for the relevant predictor variables (story topic, use of sources, journalist participation), while the organizational commenting policies were coded based on available policies and statements on the news websites. The set of commenting policies implemented by a particular news organization was assigned consistently to all stories sampled from that given news site. Reflecting a growing trend in the discipline, the data collection and coding combined both manual and automated, computer-assisted content analysis. This hybrid approach benefits from the advantages of each method. As Lewis, Zamith and Hermida (2013) argue, "hybrid combinations of computational and manual approaches can preserve the strengths of traditional content analysis, with its systematic rigor and contextual awareness, while maximizing the large-scale capacity of Big Data and the efficiencies of computational methods" (p. 47).

Given the primacy of news content as a stimulus for commenting in our Thread Structure Model, it seems reasonable to assume that the nature of comments will vary across different news topics, especially considering that comments are an "emotional response to the story" (Braun, 2015, p. 818). This is supported by interviews with news professionals, who regularly observe that the tone of user discussions is linked to the story topic (Diakopoulos & Naaman, 2011; Goodman, 2013). Coe and colleagues (2014) found that hard news stories were more likely than soft news stories to exhibit incivility in comments (sports being the exception). Ksiazek (2018) found variations in (in)civility across political news topics, with controversial topics (e.g., the gun control debate in the United States) predicting not only more comments but also more hostility in those comments. See Table 3.1 for specific story topics that predicted more/less civility and hostility in user comments.

In addition to story topic, the sources used in a given story also explain variations in comment (in)civility. Research suggests the inclusion of sources as a journalistic practice is positively related to more hostility in user comments (Ksiazek, 2018). However, it seems that the use of sources, as a general practice, is less important than the actual sources quoted. The decision to comment and the tone of that comment is likely to stem from a cognitive and emotional reaction to the source itself. In fact, Coe and colleagues (2014) found variations in incivility depending on the specific source quoted in a story. For instance, in that study stories with quotes from Barack Obama had more incivility in the user comments.

Research has also considered the role of journalist participation in comment threads. Despite concerns about intruding on "user" space (Diakopoulos & Naaman, 2011; Robinson, 2010) and the increased demand on journalists' time in order to participate (Diakopoulos & Naaman, 2011), when journalists contribute comments to these discussions we see more comments, overall, and those comments tend to be less hostile (Ksiazek, 2018). In terms of general engagement (i.e., the volume of comments), perhaps users see participation by journalists as an indicator of the value of commenting on news stories. It is also possible that users see this as an opportunity to directly interact with professional journalists, something that was previously relegated to letters to the editor and news talk radio. Regarding the improved civility of discussions where journalists contribute, this finding seems to support a surveillance effect where users are more likely to act in a civil manner if they are aware that journalists are monitoring their comments. Despite this, our analysis of commentary removal statements identified concerns about prejudicial sentiments specifically directed at journalists as one reason for removing comment sections (see Chapter 6). So, while empirical research supports a positive relationship between journalist participation in comment threads and comment civility, news organizations and journalists continue to express concerns about "author abuse" from commenters (e.g., Chen et al., 2018; Pritchard, 2016, March 26; Wolfgang, 2018). Perhaps this is why journalists only rarely engage in the practice of interacting directly with commenters (see Chapter 1): only 2.8% of the 1,379 stories in Ksiazek's (2018) analysis included journalists posting comments.

Organizational commenting policies also predict (in)civility. News organizations typically have specific policies governing their comment sections, and many of these are designed to encourage civil commentary. These policies often include required user registration, profanity filters, as well as more active pre- and post-moderation strategies, prohibiting anonymous usernames, and allowing users to rate and rank each other's comments (Domingo, 2011; Ksiazek, 2018). Research has explored the implementation of various combinations of these policies, as well as their effectiveness in predicting more civil comments (Braun, 2015; Coe et al., 2014; Ksiazek, 2015, 2018; Ruiz et al., 2011; Santana, 2014). Each of the aforementioned policies has demonstrated a positive relationship with civil commenting independently. However, when we account for these policies collectively, and control for other explanatory variables (story topic, use of sources, journalist participation), the following policies predicted more civil and/or less hostile comments: pre-moderation, post-moderation, reputation management (i.e., allowing users to police themselves through rating/ranking systems), explicitly prohibiting anonymity, and third-party user registration (where users are required to disclose publicly identifiable social cues by registering with third-party credentials, e.g., Facebook or Twitter) (Ksiazek, 2018). We will return to a more expansive treatment of organizational commenting policies in Chapter 5. For now, we move to a discussion of viewpoint diversity, where incivility might discourage users from engaging in multifaceted debate.

Viewpoint diversity

Deliberation requires that diverse viewpoints exist and that they can be uttered freely (within the confinements of law in democratic societies). One scholarly hope connected to the commentary feature as an element of participatory journalism was that ordinary people could now contribute different perspectives when they interpret and publicly discuss news (see Chapter 1). The contribution of audiences' "follow-up" or "talk back" communication to the diversity of viewpoints in news-mediated public debates has been investigated in recent years (e.g., Baden & Springer, 2014; Blassnig, Engesser, Ernst, & Esser, 2019; Toepfl & Piwoni, 2015). Similarly, scholars have engaged in researching viewpoint diversity *within* comment spaces (e.g., Douai & Nofal, 2012; Ruiz et al., 2011; see also the passage on commenters' profiles in Chapter 2). In the following, we will shed more light on both aspects.

The conditions for the representation of viewpoint diversity in comment spaces seem to be good, if we assume that diversity in public debates is likely to increase with the number of participants. For instance, a (comparative) sample of 15,314 comments analyzed by Ruiz and colleagues (2011, p. 475) "were produced by 12,309 nicknames." While it is unclear whether some commenters use several nicknames at the same time, it is still highly likely that many of these represent individuals. However, research suggests that user comments acknowledging or presenting different stances *within* their contributions most likely only happens occasionally (Douai & Nofal, 2012, p. 272; Haim,

Heinzel, Lankheit, Niagu, & Springer, 2019), and expectations that users would change their opinions over time will probably rarely be met (Toepfl & Piwoni, 2015, p. 482; see also Springer, 2014).

When focusing on viewpoint diversity and assuming that every user can contribute with their ("one-sided") opinion somehow uniquely to a debate (see Chapter 2), that most people only contribute once is not further problematic (it becomes so, however, once we focus on the act of deliberation itself, which requires interaction with divergent stances). Scholars' disappointment comes with the argumentative depth and engagement of the individual contributions (e.g., Ruiz et al., 2011), most likely if they have high normative expectations. In this regard, Slavtcheva-Petkova (2016) points out thoughtfully that lower levels of democratization and "weaker" civil societies should be taken into account when comparatively "evaluating the democratic 'reality' of online discussion" (p. 1118). For some media, however, the findings are quite promising. For instance, in their comparative study, Ruiz and colleagues (2011, p. 477) found that the New York Times and the British Guardian had "the most argumentative participants and most diverse contributors" (see also Graham & Wright, 2015). On that UK website, around one-fourth of the analyzed comments challenged "the majoritarian leftist profile of their readers, openly defending neoliberal solutions in the economic debates" (Ruiz et al., 2011, p. 477). A study by Douai and Nofal (2012) analyzed user comments posted to the websites of Al Jazeera television and Al Arabiya television, on news "discussing two events that took place outside the Arab world, the 'Swiss Minaret Ban' in 2005 and New York City's so-called 'Ground Zero Mosque' in 2010" (p. 271). The scholars found that in their expressed viewpoints concerning both issues, "readers of Al Arabiya.net appear to be evenly divided and torn, whereas Al Jazeera.net's readers appear less polarized" (p. 278). For the researchers, their study's results were quite "counter-intuitive" (p. 277): While commenters' opposition was more vocal on Al Arabiya, a majority of comments posted to Al Jazeera supported the ban. The authors conclude: "One way of explaining this discrepancy between reader comments and Al Jazeera's reputation is that readers may not fully share the news outlet's perspective on the event" (ibid.). Their findings suggest a pattern that was observed by other studies in other cultural and topical contexts, as well as on other media outlets: That users' framing of events diverges from the media's stances (p. 278).

The link between media type/slant, coverage, and users' reactions was more closely investigated, in the realm of populism, by Toepfl and Piwoni (2015) as well as by Blassnig and colleagues (2019). Blassnig and colleagues analyzed selected coverage and user comments on up-market, mass-market, TV, and online-only outlets in the UK, France, and Switzerland. The authors found that populist communication by political actors (and journalists) provoked not only more comments but also "prompt citizens to use populist key messages themselves in their comments" (p. 1), independent of the media type and "regardless of whether these messages are attenuated, amplified, or transmitted neutrally by the media" (p. 14). The authors conclude: "For readers who operate with populist arguments, the interpretation and embedding by the journalist is largely irrelevant; such readers mainly focus on statements by politicians" (ibid.).

That the journalistic contextualization can matter, however, was demonstrated in research by Toepfl and Piwoni (2015). The authors found that while Germany's opinion-leading online news outlets with slants "across the political spectrum" portrayed the German populist party "AfD" rather dismissively, "massive threads of user-generated comments appeared that were overwhelmingly dominated by commenters who were countering the consensual structures of mainstream mass media reporting" (p. 483). The authors classified around three quarters of the comments as "part of a (sub)counterpublic sphere" since they either countered issue-specific media frames, criticized bias introduced by power relations within media or politics, or posted comments that "strengthened the collective identity of party supporters" (p. 478). The researchers also noticed an impact of the outlets' political slants: "Counterpublic comments" accounted for 77.5% of the analyzed comments on right-leaning websites, but their share was clearly smaller on left-leaning outlets (63.0%). However, "the internal structure of counterpublic discourse...was surprisingly similar on both right- and left-leaning platforms" (p. 479). Additional comparisons showed that "counterpublic comments" posted to a tabloid website relied much less on counter-argumentation and were more emotional than those posted to the broadsheet outlets (p. 480). Summarizing their results, the scholars argue that through user commentary, "a powerful counter (sub)public sphere had emerged" (p. 482).

In a similar endeavor, Baden and Springer (2014) analyzed German news coverage on the European debt crisis and comments posted to these articles. The authors found that the "objects of news users' frame constructions deviate markedly from those presented in the news" (p. 540). While most journalistic accounts focus on structures, commenters emphasize actors (e.g., for attributing causal responsibility): News generally tends "to blame political problems on economic situations, and point at collective political actors for solutions" (p. 538), whereas commenters' focus lies "much more on agency" (p. 543). Moreover, commenters refer to problems beyond political decision making, for instance by discussing "flaws in contemporary capitalism, the needs and behaviour of the people" (p. 544). They also tap into historical analogies and popular wisdom (p. 545) and "evaluate more diversely and politically" (p. 544). However, commenters' opinions are rarely solution-oriented; their debate "remains, in most parts, reactive and critical" (p. 545). Zooming out from individual frame elements to a more abstract level, many identical frame fragments emerged in both the news coverage and user commentary (p. 543). Regression analyses support two causal interpretations: (1) user commentary "echoes the perspectives taken in the news, manipulating the relative salience of components but contributing little to diversity," and/or (2) "users systematically complement fragments and perspectives learned from news coverage elsewhere to complement a given article, increasing the diversity of views on a specific news platform, even if not of news discourse at large" (p. 544). Which of these two explanations holds seems to be dependent on the beat and context (e.g., users might not be confident and knowledgeable enough to contribute to economic news, p. 544). Based on their analyses, the authors conclude that "the relative freedom with which users pillaged news frame constructions to construct their own views documents their considerable independence from hegemonic news discourse" (p. 545; see also Douai & Nofal, 2012, p. 278).

In summary, studies suggest that a relevant share of commenting audiences are "inclined to seek politically dissimilar conversational partners" (Liang, 2014, p. 487): Disagreement and polarization, and thereby viewpoint diversity, was found to exist among commenters (e.g., Douai & Nofal, 2012; Lilienthal, Weichert, Reineck, Sehl, & Worm, 2014; Ruiz et al., 2011; Springer & Nuernbergk, 2016); however, polarization and diversity are more nuanced for commentary on some media and on some topics, as well as in some cultural contexts (Baden & Springer, 2014; Douai & Nofal, 2012; Ruiz et al., 2011; Slavtcheva-Petkova, 2016; Zhou et al., 2008). Findings suggest that comments can display cross-ideological debate and are not only replications or reproductions of media frames but also offer modifications and additions: Users challenge and render journalistic interpretations in a different light by proposing alternative interpretations, they mobilize historical analogies and popular wisdom. However, it is certainly questionable whether some of the formulated standpoints are socially desirable or beneficial for democratic discourse (e.g., Baden & Springer, 2014; Slavtcheva-Petkova, 2016; Toepfl & Piwoni, 2015).

Comments as political action

Given the research findings on viewpoint diversity, it is reasonable to assume that some commenters take critical stances toward political institutions, the "mainstream society," and the elite actors ruling it. For instance, in light of what was said about the overrepresentation of conservative stances among commenters (Chapter 2) and counterpublic comments (see section above), it makes sense to presume that specific audience segments use this tool to actively "correct" or "counterbalance" perspectives of more left-leaning journalists (e.g., Willnat & Weaver, 2014 for the US; Steindl, Lauerer, & Hanitzsch, 2017 for Germany; see also Chung, Munno, & Moritz, 2015). It might not be far-fetched to characterize some users who comment on news as "media skeptics;" such people perceive journalists and products of their work as selective and biased (Tsfati & Cappella, 2005; see e.g., Slavtcheva-Petkova, 2016; Toepfl & Piwoni, 2015). Accordingly, research shows that commenters' attacks frequently address a "lack of balance, wholeness, fairness, and objectivity" (Neurauter-Kessels, 2011, p. 202; Rabab'ah & Alali, 2020, p. 15), aiming to delegitimize the journalists' "authority, credibility and trustworthiness" (Neurauter-Kessels, 2011, p. 209).

This cognitively motivated engagement with the news and other users is a purposeful activity; commenters anticipate that their published opinions help readers to get a feeling about the "pulse of the public debate" (Douai & Nofal, 2012, p. 269), thus by commenting, they aim to influence public opinion building processes. We boldly go so far as to characterize such a form of commenting as digital activism or social media activism (Gerbaudo & Treré, 2015), and thereby as a form of political action. The intent of these commenters is to voice their opinions to (1) *raise awareness* about the relevance of issues or standpoints, especially if they feel that these are neglected in public discourses, and (2) to *mobilize*.

Awareness. Comment spaces are new, alternative 'public spaces' (Slavtcheva-Petkova, 2016, p. 1131) that allow users to publicly discuss or challenge democratic institutions (e.g., the state of the media), the logics in which they operate, as well as the perceived hegemonic public opinion that is also mediated by legacy media outlets. Quite conveniently, such media critiques can be directly posted onto news websites; also broader elite critiques can piggyback on the websites' reach. There may be hope among commenters that elites can be influenced by these critiques, and that critical comments can also have an impact on journalists (e.g., in their agenda setting function). For instance,

Slavtcheva-Petkova (2016) found that the commenters' (public) agenda and the media agenda can differ quite considerably: "(a) Readers have reordered the salience of the topics—they devote more attention to topics deemed less interesting by the media. (b) Readers put forward new topics" (p. 1127). Moreover, users also voice perceptions of problematic political developments, such as threats to democratic and constitutional freedoms (e.g., Douai & Nofal, 2012).

Mobilization. By raising awareness, the viewpoints in such comments become more visible and thus "louder" because of their reach: while personal communication has a natural border that ends with one's contacts, the commentary feature can facilitate communication among people who do not personally know each other, living all over a country, even all over the world, but sharing the same attitudes. That a minority can gain confidence to powerfully voice their divergent viewpoint was demonstrated by Toepfl and Piwoni (2015). In their sample, the authors found that approximately three quarters of comments supported (standpoints of) a populist party that "days before only 4.7% of the electorate had voted for" (p. 482). They conclude that their findings "showcased how an emergent collective of counterpublic-minded individuals were exploiting the comment sections of Germany's opinion-leading news websites in order to create a highly visible—and therefore enormously powerful—counterpublic sphere" (ibid.). Especially in research on populist communication, commentary features had been expected to "serve as a means to collaborate with like-minded others to advance specific ideological goals" (Blassnig et al., 2019, p. 4). Mobilizing elements in populist communication include references to ingroup (e.g., identity, deprivation) and outgroup constructions (e.g., threat), as well as emotionality (such as anger or hope; see Blassnig et al., 2019 for a summary). While such viewpoints, especially in regard to their outgroup concepts, are often considered problematic, the study by Blassnig and colleagues (2019) also indicates that populist comments "can indeed lead to arguments that may be considered as deliberative. Thus, citizens may also formulate legitimate criticism in a populist way" (p. 15).

It seems appropriate to take a step back here and offer a broader perspective on how a good deal of what we have discussed about commenters' personal characteristics informs their motivations (Chapter 2) that, in turn, can lead to gratifications discussed in Chapter 2 and in the current section. In Figure 3.1, we offer a visual representation of these interrelationships, focusing on those personal characteristics, motivations, and gratifications that appear globally generalizable. Internet efficacy and political interest are consistently identified when

Figure 3.1 Personal characteristics inform motives that can lead to gratifications.

profiling the personal characteristics of commenters. These characteristics inform cognitive and personal-identity related drivers, as well as interactive and affective motivations. These motivations, in turn, can lead to gratifications regarding personal reputation and agenda advancement, socialization, as well as the mobilizing potential of comments discussed in the preceding passages.

Anonymity certainly plays a role in these mobilization and amplification processes (we will delve deeper into anonymity in Chapter 4). Generally speaking, it is on the one hand suspected that anonymity is not only fostering incivility but also the infectious spreading of discriminating opinions. This is because people do not need to fear sanctions in their "real lives." They feel safe to utter what they might be hesitant to say in their "offline world" (e.g., Springer, 2014). On the other hand, this liberating force of anonymity can have positive effects, too, for instance in the light of the (de-)marginalization of minorities, but also to protect the voice of people living in authoritative cultures. For instance, Douai and Nofal (2012) show how commentary features on globally accessible news outlets allow "[p]reviously marginalized groups, such as Arabic speaking expatriates living in the West and elsewhere," to "actively contribute to the expansion and globalization of the online public sphere" (p. 279). In their analysis of user comments on Al Jazeera television and Al Arabiya television, the authors noticed that the "comments' language and tenor reflect a greater degree of openness, spontaneity and lesser control, aspects remarkably absent from political life in the Arab world" (ibid.). Commentary features that allow for anonymous (or at least pseudonymous) contributions can enable ordinary people to challenge instances of authoritarian control. In such participatory spaces, "Arab regimes become as vulnerable and subject to criticism as other foreign countries" (ibid.).

In addition to individual users' use and misuse of commenting features, anonymity also provides a cover for the strategic use and misuse of commentary features to influence public opinions motivated by political or commercial interests—be it manually or automated (e.g., Soffer & Gordoni, 2019, p. 14). Here, measures are applied to intentionally make opinions appear more popular than such viewpoints actually are—and also specific narratives (language, terms, and ideas) more socially acceptable. While it is certainly disputable where the legitimate usage ends and misuse begins, this line can clearly be drawn in cases where comments are spread automatically or by paid-for individuals and agencies to promote specific agendas and narratives. It has long been suspected that this form of misuse is highly prevalent (e.g., Tenenboim & Cohen, 2015, p. 214). For instance, the so-called "Russian troll army" as a means of "information war" was discussed in the media recently (e.g., Higgins, 2016). Similar activities had been observed originating from China, where hired internet commentators (the so-called "50 Cent Party" or "50 Cent army") spread favorable messages about the Communist Party (e.g., King, Pan, & Roberts, 2017).

Concerted measures to manipulate public opinion and sentiment perceptions were also reported for the "Western World," for instance as propelled by right-wing organizations on Facebook pages of German news outlets (e.g., Kreißel, Ebner, Urban, & Guhl, 2018). In reaction to the amplified spread of harmful comments, civic "counter-speech" initiatives have been initiated all over the world to promote more civil and constructive discussion cultures (ibid.; Jagärhär, 2019; Ziegele, Naab, & Jost, 2019). Actors interested in influencing public opinions would not invest resources if they did not assume that user comments had an effect on others. The concept of the "spiral of silence" proposes that we observe our environment closely to assess climates of opinion on issues at stake. Users' opinions provide such social cues (e.g., Springer, 2014). Supporting this thesis, Soffer and Gordoni (2019) found that negative user comments "significantly reduce readers' estimation of public opinion support of the issue dealt with by the article and affect the perceived support of one's opinion" (p. 1). These effects were independent of whether the comments contained personal exemplification or not. Based on this finding, the authors conclude that "user comments, whether they are framed as authentic personal stories or as general claims, can become a forceful tool in the hands of those wishing to deliberately manipulate the estimate of the public opinion climate" (p. 14).

Commenting effects

Discussing the impact of comments on readers' perceptions of public opinion touches upon an important and vivid research area in studies of user comments: Understanding the effects that user commentary has on its readers. Most available studies in this area draw upon experimental settings and repeatedly show the, at least short-term, persuasive potential of comments; the contributions can have effects on readers' perceptions, evaluations and, based on these, their actions. Similarly, user contributions can have direct or indirect impact on the news producers' perceptions, assessments, and behavior. In this area, recent interview and survey studies look more generally at the effects of (especially problematic) audience feedback. Here, user comments are considered as one of the tools that audience members use to engage with newsrooms or journalists in particular.

Comments display social cues that readers perceive, process, and react upon. For instance, when high-ego-involvement users experience comments that contradict their opinions, they believe the public (and the media) is against their position (Lee, 2012). These social cues can either be accepted or resisted. Studies suggest that users follow social cues, for instance, when comments evoke a negative spillover effect on perceptions and actions. Negative (disrespectfully) criticizing comments can diminish the persuasive influence of a news article (Heinbach, Ziegele, & Quiring, 2018; Liu & McLeod, 2019; Winter, Brückner, & Krämer, 2015). Similarly, criticizing or uncivil comments can negatively affect the perception of an article's quality (Kümpel & Springer, 2016; Prochazka, Weber, & Schweiger, 2018). Another study indicated that people's exposure to prejudiced comments led them to post more prejudiced comments themselves (Hsueh, Yogeeswaran, & Malinen, 2015). Studies also find positive spillover effects. For instance, positive comments can lead to a more favorable assessment regarding the perceived public opinion climate, responsibility attribution, and attitudinal evaluations of a financial manager scandalized by the news (von Sikorski & Hänelt, 2016). Moreover, comments appraising journalistic quality were shown to positively impact readers' quality assessments (Kümpel & Springer, 2016).

However, audiences might also be quite resistant toward user commentary. The processing of comments seems to be influenced by the recipients' predispositions and relevance of the topic (e.g., Anderson, Brossard, Scheufele, Xenos, & Ladwig, 2014; Winter et al., 2015) but also by the comments' substance. For instance, Chen and Ng (2016) showed that participants exposed to civil comments presumed their influence on the opinions of others to be clearly higher than participants exposed to uncivil comments. According to recent research, it is also suspected that user comments' effects on their readers are rather short lived. A study by Heinbach, Ziegele and Quiring (2018) shows that, when (re-)measured after two weeks, the impact of comments on an article's persuasiveness "had disappeared, whereas the article's arguments still had an impact on the attitudes of the participants compared to a control group" (p. 4780). The authors suggest that this result can stem from different reading modes: while the article's arguments might have been processed more thoroughly, other information, such as accompanying user comments, more heuristically (ibid.).

Nevertheless, the sheer amount and sentiment of incoming user feedback can leave quite an impression, especially on news professionals. We touched on the indirect effects of comments on journalists' production routines in Chapter 1: it is assumed that future decisions on news selection and presentation can be impacted by high levels of audience engagement with specific content; for instance, "if populism generates a high user response, it may be beneficial from a commercial viewpoint for the media to cite or voice such messages in their content" (Blassnig et al., 2019, p. 15). Recently, studies have focused more and more on the consequences of problematic, threatening, and harassing audience feedback, such as abusive comments (e.g., Adams, 2018; Chen et al., 2018; Löfgren Nilsson & Örnebring, 2016; Obermaier, Hofbauer, & Reinemann, 2018; Post & Kepplinger, 2019; Stahel & Schoen, 2019). These consequences can be both personal and professional: emotional reactions and impact on the journalists' wellbeing, avoidance of interactions with the audience and tendencies toward self-censorship (e.g., decisions to avoid reporting on specific topics, subjects, and groups to elude anticipated hostility). Findings suggest that the more frequently journalists are attacked, the more self-censorship they exert (Löfgren Nilsson & Örnebring, 2016, p. 887).

Research on how commenting affects journalists has also explored gender differences: female journalists were found to be more likely to "avoid attacks by limiting their engagement with audiences, adapting their reporting behavior, and considering quitting journalism" (Stahel & Schoen, 2019, p. 15) because they feel more stressed by attacks (ibid.; see also Post & Kepplinger, 2019). Hateful comments can thus be considered a threat to diversity in newsrooms (see also Gardiner et al., 2016). However, female journalists were also found to manage a positive reframing of the consequences that problematic audience feedback has on their work routines: anticipated pressure can result in more accurate and considerate reporting, for instance, to include "all voices" and take publication effects into account (Chen et al., 2018, p. 11).

To summarize, the literature on commenting effects shows that user comments serve the audience as information for what others think about controversial topics and mainstream media coverage in general and that they have the potential for at least short-term influence, such as affecting the audience's perception of journalistic quality. Moreover, harmful comments' consequences on journalists' wellbeing and work routines are concerning. Thus, user comments' relevance cannot be ignored, and the improvement of user discussions' civility becomes an urgent matter.

Beyond deliberation

To this point, Habermas's deliberative model has been the dominant framework in commenting research. But, given contextually situated understandings of (in)civility, we should also consider variations in commenting norms, beyond just deliberation. For instance, Freelon (2015) argues that online political discussions might also be characterized by communitarianism (i.e., "collaborating with like-minded others to advance ideologically specific goals and disengaging with outsiders") and liberal individualism (i.e., "the single-minded pursuit of uninhibited self-expression, usually at the expense of civility and responsiveness") (p. 774). The latter would clearly alter our understanding of civility and hostility in user comments, and Freelon found evidence that "newspaper comment sections are spaces of both liberal individualism and deliberation" (p. 785).

Quandt (2018) makes a case for increased conceptual and empirical attention on "dark participation." Unlike the more utopic view that civil commentary will in some way contribute to the health of the public sphere and deliberative democracy, dark participation refers to the social reality that a great deal of user commentary is motivated by or characterized as intentional misinformation, hate campaigns, trolling, and cyberbullying. In fact, research suggests that "angry" people are more likely to engage in social media discussions about politics (Wollebæk, Karlsen, Steen-Johnsen, & Enjolras, 2019). Quandt argues that these "dark" forms of public engagement with the news are equally deserving of our scholarly attention.

Despite these alternative conceptualizations, recent cutting-edge research on the use of artificial intelligence to manage user comments has focused on how machine learning can be applied in identifying and processing good (i.e., constructive, argumentative) user contributions. Scholars working in this research area are still drawing (implicitly and explicitly) on deliberation theory to identify what constitutes such "good" and "constructive" commentary (e.g., the classifier "arguments used" by Schabus and colleagues (2017, p. 1242) explores the automated detection of comments that "back their statements with rational argumentation, reasoning and sources"). This signals the continued relevance of a deliberation framework, despite its limitations.

With the deliberative potential of comments as public engagement serving as a backdrop, the final chapter engages the debate around whether the field of digital journalism should abandon comments (where organizations often cite various forms of "dark participation") or find ways to encourage more productive commentary by critically assessing and reflecting on currently insufficient moderation strategies (e.g., those that are focused on policing and banning instead of being engaging and encouraging). Before that, we first discuss the disruptive role of anonymity in commenting and the relationship between anonymity and engagement/civility (Chapter 4) and then turn to a discussion of organizational policies and moderation practices for managing and improving the quality of user commentary (Chapter 5).

References

Adams, C. (2018). They go for gender first. *Journalism Practice, 12*(7), 850–869. doi: 10.1080/17512786.2017.1350115

Alonzo, M., & Aiken, M. (2004). Flaming in electronic communication. *Decision Support Systems, 36*, 205–213. doi: 10.1016/S0167-9236(02)00190-2

Anderson, A. A., Brossard, D., Scheufele, D. A., Xenos, M. A., & Ladwig, P. (2014). The "nasty effect:" Online incivility and risk perceptions of emerging technologies. *Journal of Computer-Mediated Communication, 19*(3), 373–387. doi: 10.1111/jcc4.12009

Baden, C., & Springer, N. (2014). Com(ple)menting the news on the financial crisis: The contribution of news users' commentary to the diversity of viewpoints in the public debate. *European Journal of Communication, 29*(5), 529–548. doi: 10.1177/0267323114538724

Barnes, R. (2015). Understanding the affective investment produced through commenting on Australian alternative journalism website New Matilda. *New Media & Society, 17*(5), 810–826. doi: 10.1177/1461444813511039

Benson, T. W. (1996). Rhetoric, civility, and community: Political debate on computer bulletin boards. *Communication Quarterly, 44*(3), 359–378. doi: 10.1080/01463379609370023

Blassnig, S., Engesser, S., Ernst, N., & Esser, F. (2019). Hitting a nerve: Populist news articles lead to more frequent and more populist reader comments. *Political Communication*. Advance Online Publication. doi: 10.1080/10584609.2019.1637980

Boczkowski, P. J., & Mitchelstein, E. (2012). How users take advantage of different forms of interactivity on online news sites: Clicking, e-mailing, and commenting. *Human Communication Research, 38*(1), 1–22. doi: 10.1111/j.1468–2958.2011.01418.x

Braun, J. A. (2015). News programs: Designing MSNBC.com's online interfaces. *Journalism, 16*(1), 27–43. doi: 10.1177/1464884914545730

Chen, G. M., & Ng, Y. M. M. (2016). Third-person perception of online comments: Civil ones persuade you more than me. *Computers in Human Behavior, 55*, 736–742. doi: 10.1016/j.chb.2015.10.014

Chen, G. M., Pain, P., Chen, V. Y., Mekelburg, M., Springer, N., & Troger, F. (2018). 'You really have to have a thick skin': A cross-cultural perspective on how online harassment influences female journalists. *Journalism*. Advance Online Publication. doi: 10.1177/1464884918768500

Chung, M., Munno, G. J., & Moritz, B. (2015). Triggering participation: Exploring the effects of third-person and hostile media perceptions on online participation. *Computers in Human Behavior, 53*, 452–461. doi: 10.1016/j.chb.2015.06.037

Coe, K., Kenski, K., & Rains, S. A. (2014). Online and uncivil? Patterns and determinants of incivility in newspaper website comments. *Journal of Communication, 64*, 658–679. doi: 10.1111/jcom.12104

Diakopoulos, N., & Naaman, M. (2011). Towards quality discourse in online news comments. *Proceedings of CSCW 2011* (pp. 133–142). March 19–23, Hangzhou, China. doi: 10.1145/1958824.1958844

Díaz Noci, J., Domingo, D., Masip, P., Lluís Micó, J., & Ruiz, C. (2010). Comments in news, democracy booster or journalistic nightmare: Assessing the quality and dynamics of citizen debates in Catalan online newspapers. *International Symposium on Online Journalism*. Austin. April 23–24.

Domingo, D. (2011). Managing audience participation. Practices, workflows and strategies. In J. B. Singer, A. Hermida, D. Domingo, A. Heinonen, S. Paulussen, T. Quandt, … (Eds.), *Participatory journalism. Guarding open gates at online newspapers* (pp. 76–95). Sussex: Wiley-Blackwell.

Douai, A., & Nofal, H. K. (2012). Commenting in the online Arab public sphere: Debating the Swiss minaret ban and the "Ground Zero Mosque" online. *Journal of Computer-Mediated Communication, 17*(3), 266–282. doi: 10.1111/j.1083-6101.2012.01573.x

Ferree, M. M., Gamson, W. A., Gerhards, J., & Rucht, D. (2002). Four models of the public sphere in modern democracies. *Theory and Society, 31*, 289–324. doi: 10.1023/A:1016284431021

Freelon, D. (2015). Discourse architecture, ideology, and democratic norms in online political discussion. *New Media & Society, 17*(5), 772–791. doi: 10.1177/1461444813513259

Gardiner, B., Mansfield, M., Anderson, I., Holder, J., Louter, D., & Ulmanu, M. (2016, 12. April). The dark side of Guardian comments. *The Guardian*. Retrieved from https://www.theguardian.com/technology/2016/apr/12/the-dark-side-of-guardian-comments (accessed 12 December 2019).

Gerbaudo, P., & Treré, E. (2015). In search of the 'we' of social media activism: Introduction to the special issue on social media and protest identities. *Information, Communication & Society, 18*(8), 865–871. doi: 10.1080/1369118X.2015.1043319

Goodman, E. (2013). Online comment moderation: Emerging best practices. *World Association of Newspapers (WAN-IFRA)*. Retrieved from http://www.wan-ifra.org/reports/2013/10/04/online-comment-moderation-emerging-best-practices

Graham, T., & Wright, S. (2015). A tale of two stories from "Below the Line" comment fields at the Guardian. *The International Journal of Press/Politics, 20*(3), 317–338. doi: 10.1177/1940161215581926

Habermas, J. (1989). *The structural transformation of the public sphere: An inquiry into a category of bourgeois society.* Cambridge: MIT Press.

Haim, M., Heinzel, I., Lankheit, S., Niagu, A. M., & Springer, N. (2019, May). *Identifying the good and the bad: Using machine learning to moderate user commentary on news.* Paper presentation at the annual International Communication Association (ICA) conference, Washington, DC.

Hardaker, C. (2010). Trolling in asynchronous computer-mediated communication: From user discussions to academic definitions. *Journal of Politeness Research, 6*, 215–242. doi: 10.1515/JPLR.2010.011

Heinbach, D., Ziegele, M., & Quiring, O. (2018). Sleeper effect from below. Long-term effects of source credibility and user comments on the persuasiveness of news articles. *New Media & Society, 20*(18), 4765–4786. doi: 10.1177/1461444818784472

Herbst, S. (2010). *Rude democracy: Civility and incivility in American politics.* Philadelphia: Temple University Press.

Higgins, A. (2016, May 31). Effort to expose Russia's 'troll army' draws vicious retaliation. *The New York Times.* Retrieved from www.nytimes.com/2016/05/31/world/europe/russia-finland-nato-trolls.html?_r=1 (accessed 12 December 2019).

Himelboim, I. (2011). Civil society and online political discourse: The network structure of unrestricted discussion. *Communication Research, 38*, 634–659. doi: 10.1177/0093650210384853

Hsueh, M., Yogeeswaran, K., & Malinen, S. (2015). "Leave your comment below": Can biased online comments influence our own prejudicial attitudes and behaviors? *Human Communication Research, 41*(4), 557–576. doi: 10.1111/hcre.12059

Hurrell, A. C. (2005). Civility in online discussion: The case of foreign policy dialogue. *Canadian Journal of Communication, 30*, 633–648. Retrieved from http://www.cjc-online.ca/index.php/journal/article/view/1585

Jagärhär (2019, January 27). The #iamhere network. Retrieved from https://www.jagarhar.se/kolumnen/the-iamhere-network/

Jamieson, K. H., Volinsky, A., Weitz, I., & Kenski, K. (2017). The political uses and abuses of civility and incivility. In K. Kenski & K. H. Jamieson (Eds.), *The Oxford handbook of political communication.* New York: Oxford University Press. doi: 10.1093/oxfordhb/9780199793471.013.79_update_001

King, G., Pan, J., & Roberts, M. E. (2017). How the Chinese government fabricates social media posts for strategic distraction, not engaged argument. *American Political Science Review, 111*(3), 484–501. doi: 10.1017/S0003055417000144

Kreißel, P., Ebner, J., Urban, A., & Guhl, J. (2018). *Hass auf Knopfdruck.* Rechtsextreme Trollfabriken und das Ökosystem koordinierter Hasskampagnen im Netz. Institute for Strategic Dialogue. London. Retrieved from https://www.isdglobal.org/wp-content/uploads/2018/07/ISD_Ich_Bin_Hier_2.pdf (accessed 12 December 2019).

Ksiazek, T. B. (2015). Civil interactivity: How news organizations' commenting policies explain civility and hostility in user comments. *Journal of Broadcasting & Electronic Media, 59*(4), 556–573. doi: 10.1080/08838151.2015.1093487

Ksiazek, T. B. (2018). Commenting on the news: Explaining the degree and quality of user comments on news websites. *Journalism Studies, 19*(5), 650–673. doi: 10.1080/1461670X.2016.1209977

Ksiazek, T. B., & Peer, L. (2016). User comments and civility on YouTube. In B. Franklin & S.A. Eldridge II (Eds.), *Routledge companion to digital journalism studies* (pp. 244–252). New York: Routledge.

Ksiazek, T. B., Peer, L., & Zivic, A. (2015). Discussing the news: Civility and hostility in user comments. *Digital Journalism, 3*(6), 850–870. doi: 10.1080/21670811.2014.972079

Kümpel, A., & Springer, N. (2016). Commenting quality. Effects of user comments on perceptions of journalistic quality. *Studies in Communication and Media, 5*(3), 353–366. doi: 10.5771/2192-4007-2016-3-353

Lee, E. J. (2012). That's not the way it is: How user-generated comments on the news affect perceived media bias. *Journal of Computer-Mediated Communication, 18*(1), 32–45. doi: 10.1111/j.1083–6101.2012.01597.x

Lee, H. (2005). Behavioral strategies for dealing with flaming in an online forum. *The Sociological Quarterly, 46*(2), 385–403. doi: 10.1111/j.1533-8525.2005.00017.x

Lewis, S. C., Zamith, R., & Hermida, A. (2013). Content analysis in an era of big data: A hybrid approach to computational and manual methods. *Journal of Broadcasting and Electronic Media, 57*(1), 34–52. doi: 10.1080/08838151.2012.761702

Liang, H. (2014). The organizational principles of online political discussion: A relational event stream model for analysis of web forum deliberation. *Human Communication Research, 40*(4), 483–507. doi: 10.1111/hcre.12034

Lilienthal, V., Weichert, S., Reineck, D., Sehl, A., & Worm, S. (2014). *Digitaler Journalismus. Dynamik – Teilhabe – Technik.* Leipzig: Vistas.

Liu, J., & McLeod, D. M. (2019). Counter-framing effects of user comments. *International Journal of Communication, 13*, 2484–2503. Retrieved from https://ijoc.org/index.php/ijoc/article/view/11392

Löfgren Nilsson, M., & Örnebring, H. (2016). Journalism under threat: Intimidation and harassment of Swedish journalists. *Journalism Practice, 10*(7), 880–890. doi: 10.1080/17512786.2016.1164614

Meltzer, K. (2015). Journalistic concern about uncivil political talk in digital news media: Responsibility, credibility, and academic influence. *The International Journal of Press/Politics, 20*(1), 85–107. doi: 10.1177/1940161214558748

Moor, P. J., Heuvelman, A., & Verleur, R. (2010). Flaming on YouTube. *Computers in Human Behavior, 26*, 1536–1546. doi: 10.1016/j.chb.2010.05.023

Neurauter-Kessels, M. (2011). Im/polite reader responses on British online news sites. *Journal of Politeness Research, 7*, 187–214. doi: 10.1515/JPLR.2011.010

Ng, E. W. J., & Detenber, B. H. (2005). The impact of synchronicity and civility in online political discussions on perceptions and intentions to participate. *Journal of Computer Mediated Communication, 10*(3), article 4. Retrieved from http://jcmc.indiana.edu/vol10/issue3/ng.html

Nielsen, C. E. (2012). Newspaper journalists support online comments. *Newspaper Research Journal, 33*(1), 86–100. doi: 10.1177/073953291203300107

Obermaier, M., Hofbauer, M., & Reinemann, C. (2018). Journalists as targets of hate speech How German journalists perceive the consequences for themselves and how they cope with it. *Studies in Communication and Media, 7*(4), 499–524, doi: 10.5771/2192–4007-2018-4-499

O'Sullivan, P. B., & Flanagin, A. J. (2003). Reconceptualizing "flaming" and other problematic messages. *New Media and Society, 5*(1), 69–94. doi: 10.1177/1461444803005001908

Papacharissi, Z. (2004). Democracy online: Civility, politeness, and the democratic potential of online political discussion groups. *New Media & Society, 6*(2), 259–283. doi: 10.1177/1461444804041444

Pennebaker, J. W., Booth, R. J., & Francis, M. E. (2007). *Linguistic inquiry and word count (LIWC): LIWC2007.* LIWC, Inc. Retrieved from http://www.liwc.net

Post, S., & Kepplinger, H. M. (2019). Coping with audience hostility. How journalists' experiences of audience hostility influence their editorial decisions. *Journalism Studies.* Advance Online Publication. doi: 10.1080/1461670X.2019.1599725

Pritchard, S. (2016, March 26). The readers' editor on…closing comments below the line. *The Guardian.* Retrieved from https://www.theguardian.com/commentisfree/2016/mar/27/readers-editor-on-closing-comments-below-line

Prochazka, F., Weber, P., & Schweiger, W. (2018). Effects of civility and reasoning in user comments on perceived journalistic quality. *Journalism Studies, 19*(1), 62–78. doi: 10.1080/1461670X.2016.1161497

Quandt, T. (2018). Dark participation. *Media and Communication, 6*(4), 36–48. doi: 10.17645/mac.v6i4.1519

Rabab'ah, G., & Alali, N. (2020). Impoliteness in reader comments on the Al-Jazeera Channel news website. *Journal of Politeness Research, 16*(1), 1–43. doi: 10.1515/pr-2017–0028

Reader, B. (2012). Free press vs. free speech? The rhetoric of 'civility' in regard to anonymous online comments. *Journalism & Mass Communication Quarterly, 89*, 495–513. doi: 10.1177/1077699012447923

Richardson, J. E., & Stanyer, J. (2011). Reader opinion in the digital age: Tabloid and broadsheet newspaper websites and the exercise of political voice. *Journalism, 12*(8), 983–1003. doi: 10.1177/1464884911415974

Robinson, S. (2010). Traditionalists vs. convergers: Textual privilege, boundary work, and the journalist—Audience relationship in the commenting policies of online news sites. *Convergence: The International Journal of Research into New Media Technologies, 16*(1), 125–143. doi: 10.1177/1354856509347719

Ruiz, C., Domingo, D., Micó, J. L., Díaz-Noci, J., Meso, K., & Masip, P. (2011). Public sphere 2.0? The democratic qualities of citizen debates in online newspapers. *The International Journal of Press/Politics, 16*(4), 463–487. doi: 10.1177/1940161211415849

Santana, A. D. (2011). Online readers' comments represent new opinion pipeline. *Newspaper Research Journal, 32*(3), 66–81. doi: 10.1177/073953291103200306

Santana, A. D. (2014). Virtuous or vitriolic. The effect of anonymity on civility in online newspaper reader comment boards. *Journalism Practice, 8*(1), 18–33. doi: 10.1080/17512786.2013.813194

Schabus, D., Skowron, M., & Trapp, M. (2017). One million posts: A data set of German online discussions. *Proceedings of the 40th International ACM SIGIR Conference on Research and Development in Information Retrieval (SIGIR)* (pp. 1241–1244). August 7–11, Tokyo, Japan. doi: 10.1145/3077136.3080711

Schudson, M. (1997). Why conversation is not the soul of democracy. *Critical Studies in Mass Communication, 14*(4), 297–309. doi: 10.1080/15295039709367020

Sifianou, M. (2019). Im/politeness and in/civility: A neglected relationship? *Journal of Pragmatics, 147*, 49–64. doi: 10.1016/j.pragma.2019.05.008

Slavtcheva-Petkova, V. (2016). Are newspapers' online discussion boards democratic tools or conspiracy theories' engines? A case study on an Eastern European "media war." *Journalism & Mass Communication Quarterly, 93*(4), 1115–1134. doi: 10.1177/1077699015610880

Soffer, O., & Gordoni, G. (2019). The role of user comments in estimation of the public opinion climate and perceived support for one's opinion. *International Journal of Public Opinion Research.* Advance Online Publication. doi: 10.1093/ijpor/edz036

Springer, N. (2014). *Beschmutzte Öffentlichkeit? Warum Menschen die Kommentarfunktion auf Online-Nachrichtenseiten als öffentliche Toilettenwand benutzen, warum Besucher ihre Hinterlassenschaften trotzdem lesen, und wie die Wände im Anschluss aussehen.* Berlin: LIT Verlag Münster.

Springer, N., Engelmann, I., & Pfaffinger, C. (2015). User comments: Motives and inhibitors to write and read. *Information, Communication & Society, 18*(7), 798–815. doi: 10.1080/1369118X.2014.997268

Springer, N., & Nuernbergk, C. (2016, June). *Commenting user networks: Two case studies on interactions and behavioral self-regulation in comments sections.* Paper presentation at the annual International Communication Association (ICA) conference, Fukuoka, Japan.

Stahel, L., & Schoen, C. (2019). Female journalists under attack? Explaining gender differences in reactions to audiences' attacks. *New Media & Society.* Advance Online Publication. doi: 10.1177/1461444819885333

Steindl, N., Lauerer, C., & Hanitzsch, T. (2017). Journalismus in Deutschland. Aktuelle Befunde zu Kontinuität und Wandel im deutschen Journalismus. *Publizistik, 62*, 401–423. doi: 10.1007/s11616-017-0378-9

Taneja, H., Webster, J. G., Malthouse, E. C., & Ksiazek, T. B. (2012). Media consumption across platforms: Identifying user-defined repertoires. *New Media & Society, 14*(6), 951–968. doi: 10.1177/1461444811436146

Tenenboim, O., & Cohen, A. A. (2015). What prompts users to click and comment: A longitudinal study of online news. *Journalism, 16*(2), 198–217. doi: 10.1177/1464884913513996

Toepfl, F., & Piwoni, E. (2015). Public spheres in interaction: Comment sections of news websites as counterpublic spaces. *Journal of Communication, 65*(3), 465–488. doi: 10.1111/jcom.12156

Tsfati, Y., & Cappella, J. N. (2005). Why do people watch news they do not trust? The need for cognition as a moderator in the association between news media skepticism and exposure. *Media Psychology, 7*(3), 251–271. doi: 10.1207/S1532785XMEP0703_2

Turnage, A. K. (2007). Email flaming behaviors and organizational conflict. *Journal of Computer-Mediated Communication, 13*, 43–59. doi: 10.1111/j.1083-6101.2007.00385.x

von Sikorski, C., & Hänelt, M. (2016). Scandal 2.0: How valenced reader comments affect recipients' perception of scandalized individuals and the journalistic quality of online news. *Journalism & Mass Communication Quarterly, 93*(3), 551–571. doi: 10.1177/1077699016628822

Willnat, L., & Weaver, D. H. 2014. The American journalist in the digital age: Key findings. Retrieved from https://larswillnat.files.wordpress.com/2014/05/2013-american-journalist-key-findings.pdf (accessed 12 December 2019).

Winter S., Brückner, C., & Krämer, N. C. (2015). They came, they liked, they commented: Social influence on Facebook news channels. *Cyberpsychology, Behavior, and Social Networking, 18*(8), 431–436. doi: 10.1089/cyber.2015.0005

Wolfgang, J. D. (2018). Cleaning up the "fetid swamp:" Examining how journalists construct policies and practices for moderating comments. *Digital Journalism, 6*(1), 21–40. doi: 10.1080/21670811.2017.1343090

Wollebæk, D., Karlsen, R., Steen-Johnsen, K., & Enjolras, B. (2019). Anger, fear, and echo chambers: The emotional basis for online behavior. *Social Media + Society, 5*(2), 1–14. doi: 10.1177/2056305119829859

Zhou, X., Chan, Y. Y., & Peng, Z. M. (2008). Deliberativeness of online political discussion. *Journalism Studies, 9*(5), 759–770. doi: 10.1080/14616700802207771

Ziegele, M., Naab, T. K., & Jost, P. (2019). Lonely together? Identifying the determinants of collective corrective action against uncivil comments. *New Media & Society*. Advance Online Publication. doi: 1461444819870130

4 Anonymous commentary

In this chapter, we engage the current debate around anonymity in user comments. While anonymity was the norm in the very earliest letters to the editor (Reader, 2015), anonymous user comments disrupt digital journalism by contradicting contemporary ethical norms in journalism regarding transparency and source attribution (Nielsen, 2012; Shanahan, 2018). Further, anonymous commenters are often blamed for the apparent pervasiveness of incivility in comments, which undermines the deliberative potential of comment spaces, and many news organizations now require commenters to be identifiable. We elaborate on the disruptive nature of anonymity, stemming from an "online disinhibition effect" (Suler, 2004, 2005); offer varying perspectives and organizational approaches to anonymity; and integrate our empirical work on the relationships between anonymity and both user engagement and (in)civility (Ksiazek, 2015, 2018).

Disruptive anonymity

The observation that people seem to "behave online in ways that appear quite uninhibited as compared with their usual offline behavior" (Suler, 2005, p. 184) resulted in the formulation of a concept called "the online disinhibition effect" (Suler, 2004, 2005). This suggests that if internet users have the option to communicate anonymously, they can "detach their actions online from their in-person lifestyle and identity" and thus "feel less vulnerable about self-disclosing or acting out" (Suler, 2005, p. 185; see also Joinson, 2007). It is helpful to differentiate between three levels of 'possible detachment' in commenting, in this context: users are able to contribute *anonymously*, if no pre-registration is required, and they are free to choose a random username (however, they might still leave traceable cues for news providers, such as IP addresses; see Reich, 2011, p. 111). Users can contribute *pseudonymously*, if they are still free to choose a random username, however, have to register with valid personal information, for instance an email address ("on-site user registration," see Chapter 5). Finally, users can be required to disclose *publicly identifiable social cues*, such as their real name or a social media profile ("third-party user registration," see Chapter 5). The disinhibition effect can then be thought of as a continuum (e.g., Cho & Kwon, 2015), with disinhibition being most prevalent in the first condition (anonymous commenting) and comparatively less likely to occur in the third condition (requirement to disclose social cues). However, it is unrealistic to assume that removing anonymity would be able to eliminate incivility or hostility completely (e.g., Santana, 2014, p. 28; see Chapter 5).

Suler (2005, p. 184) differentiates two types of disinhibition: Benign and toxic disinhibition. Benign disinhibition describes, for instance, situations in which people disclose in online communication "emotions, fears, and wishes" that they keep to themselves in offline-encounters. Toxic disinhibition, in contrast is exhibited, for instance, when users communicate in a "rude, critical, angry, hateful, and threatening" way (ibid.). It has already been established in Chapter 3 that allowing for anonymous communication can give voice to suppressed groups and individuals. Here, we see benign disinhibition playing out: anonymity can cover identities of marginalized and oppressed (groups of) internet users, making their representation in commentary spaces possible by allowing them to raise awareness or to mobilize. More focus, however, is placed on toxic disinhibition—given its prevalence, threat to constructive online debate, and its potential to silence divergent opinions, for instance, of such marginalized groups.

According to Suler (2004, 2005), six (interacting) factors are responsible for the online disinhibition effect: *Dissociative anonymity*, *invisibility*, *asynchronicity*, *solipsistic introjection*, *dissociative imagination*, and *minimization of authority*. Regarding toxic disinhibition, five of these factors seem to be particularly relevant: *Dissociative anonymity* has already been introduced above: "The online self becomes a compartmentalized self, a dissociated self. In the case of expressed hostilities or other deviant acts, the person can evade responsibility…" (Suler, 2005, p. 185). *Invisibility* disinhibits users because they can avoid "eye contact and face-to-face visibility" and thus social sanctions such as signals of disapproval (ibid.). In addition, *asynchronicity* can disinhibit users because they do not have "to cope with someone's immediate reaction" (ibid.). The factor *dissociative imagination* combines the possible detachment from and a perceived 'un-realness' of the online activity. When users end their commenting session and "return to their daily routine," they might "believe they leave behind that game and their persona within" (p. 187). Research shows that some users indeed talk about their commenting activity in terms borrowed from gaming contexts (Springer, 2014). Lastly, Suler (2005) mentions *attenuated status and authority*: "Because of fear of disapproval or punishment, people are reluctant to say what they really think as they stand before an authority figure" (p. 187). Visual cues such as clothes and body language signal status in the offline-world; in text-based communication, however, such cues are absent. Hence, online communication feels more like peer-to-peer interaction—and therefore less intimidating.

Moreover, Suler (2004, 2005) also expects that *individual differences* such as traits and personality types "play an important role in determining when and how people become disinhibited" (Suler, 2005, p. 188). Findings by Wu and Atkin (2017) suggest that agreeableness and narcissism are "key personality predictors of motivations for posting comments on online news" (p. 73, see also Chapter 2). While agreeable persons are oriented and empathetic towards others, narcissistic personalities are self-oriented and attention-seeking (pp. 68–69, 74; see also Chapter 2). Similarly, a study by Buckels and colleagues (2014) suggests that "Dark Tetrad" traits—narcissism, Machiavellianism, psychopathy, and sadism—are positively associated with the frequency of commenting on websites (news sites included). More aggressive, anti-social styles of commenting can thus be expected from these types of commenters—aspects that the "dark participation" framework is able to capture (see Chapter 3). In addition, commenting behavior and commenting style, respectively, is also assumed to be impacted by cultural contexts (e.g., Rabab'ah & Alali, 2020); being conflict-ready, straight-forward, and aggressive in discussions is more acceptable in some cultures than in others (Reich, 2011, p. 104).

It is also apparent that, especially in anonymous or pseudonymous commenting conditions, "users have less face at stake and consequently less face to lose" (Neurauter-Kessels, 2011, p. 195): While many journalists "are publicly known figures and have a public reputation to defend" (p. 196), users "hide behind the anonymity that screen names afford" (Reich, 2011, p. 114) or are at least harder to identify. The publicity makes comments even more face-threatening (Neurauter-Kessels, 2011, pp. 197–198). It has been shown that, in the face of overtly aggressive, abusive audience feedback, some female technology journalists also decided to "[go] anonymous" (Adams, 2018, p. 859): "One in five women journalists surveyed said they had disguised their identity, by disguising their gender, name or publishing anonymously" (ibid.).

Anonymity, engagement, and (in)civility

Given the problematic effects that toxic disinhibition in user comments has on comment writers and readers, news producers, and the perception of their news product (see also Chapter 3), some news organizations choose to prohibit anonymity as a way to foster more civil discussion by requiring users to be identifiable for others. Santana (2014) found that US news organizations are divided in their approach to anonymity: Roughly half require identifiable usernames, while half allow anonymity. However, Ksiazek (2015, 2018) found only 4 out of 20 news organizations in his US and UK sample explicitly prohibited anonymity. Thus, it does not seem that concerns about toxic disinhibition clearly outweigh principles of online communication culture, "which developed around being anonymous" (Adams, 2018, p. 859) and encompass users' strong desire for privacy and anonymity (e.g., Kang, Brown, & Kiesler, 2013).

The logic behind a policy of prohibiting anonymity is based on the assumption—derived from the online disinhibition effect—that users who can hide behind anonymous usernames are less accountable and thus more likely to post hostile comments. In the context of our Thread Structure Model, a lack of accountability due to anonymity has the potential to disrupt user-user interactions (in terms of the quality of both discussion and dialogue), as well as user-content reactions and user-journalist interactions. In a survey of SacBee.com users (the website for the *Sacramento Bee*, a US-based news organization in Sacramento, California), Diakopoulos and Naaman (2011) found that users believed prohibiting anonymity should improve the quality of comments, and recent empirical research by Ksiazek (2015, 2018) and Santana (2014, 2019) found support for this prediction. Moreover, if anonymity leads to toxic commenting in the form of user-content reactions or user-journalist interactions, users may lose trust in a news organization and its journalists and stop using a given news website altogether.

It seems reasonable to assume that prohibiting anonymity would hold users publicly accountable for their comments, which should decrease the likelihood of posting in a hostile manner. Ksiazek (2015) analyzed the difference in hostile language between news organizations that do and do not prohibit anonymity in their comment sections, and found that news websites that had a policy of prohibiting anonymity exhibited less hostile conversation in their user comments. This finding held when controlling for other organizational commenting policies in regression models, which supported the hypothesis that prohibiting anonymity improves the quality of user commentary. It would seem that when commenters are accountable and identifiable they contribute in more productive ways and tend to eschew hostility/incivility.

Similarly, in a content analysis of 4,800 comments about the 2016 US presidential election sampled from 30 online news sites, Santana (2019) found that non-anonymous comments were more civil (61%) than anonymous comments (34%). That same study also found that several other indicators of quality deliberation were significantly more likely to be present in non-anonymous comments than anonymous ones. These include: "being...*reciprocal* in which participants acknowledge the point of view of others; *reflexive* in which the commenter is self-aware via personal and/or firsthand observations; *on-topic* and focused on the issue/news at hand; and grounded in *rationality*, expressed through reasoned argumentation" (pp. 470–471). Related, Santana (2019) also found a higher likelihood of *affective catharsis* in anonymous comments, defined as a comment that "appealed to non-factual arguments or reasoning...contained no empirical evidence to support an opinion...and was devoid of rationality or perspective" (p. 478). It is worth noting that while Ksiazek (2018) found prohibiting anonymity reduced hostility, this same policy was also related to lower levels of civility in user commentary. Clearly, more research is needed to inform generalized claims about the relationship between anonymity and (in)civility.

An increasing number of news organizations have begun to outsource commenting to third-party social media platforms in conjunction with or as a replacement for their own commenting spaces. This trend has real implications for the relationship between anonymity and (in)civility, as social media platforms necessarily discourage and/or prohibit anonymity. The requirement to publicly disclose social cues (e.g., though the login via a social network profile) is associated with less flaming in user comments (Cho & Kwon, 2015) and leads to a reduction of offensive words (Fredheim, Moore, & Naughton, 2015).

It is worth distinguishing between explicit, or direct, policies regarding anonymity and those that more indirectly manage the public disclosure of a user's identity. While some news organizations might explicitly prohibit anonymity in their commenting guidelines and policies, others do so indirectly by requiring on-site or third-party user registration (see Ksiazek, 2015, 2018; also Chapters 3 and 5). On-site user registration allows users to comment *pseudonymously*, for instance, if they are free to choose a random username but have to register with valid personal information. While users might choose to create a nickname or other pseudonymous username, they are still identifiable to the news organization. Third-party user registration requires commenters to disclose *publicly identifiable social cues*, by registering with third-party credentials (e.g., Facebook or Twitter). Here, users are more identifiable to both the news organization and other commenters. These direct/indirect anonymity policies seem to have real implications for the likelihood of toxic disinhibition in user comments, and align with the online disinhibition continuum discussed earlier. For instance, Ksiazek (2015, 2018) found that explicitly prohibiting anonymity (direct) and requiring third-party user registration (indirect) both predicted lower levels of hostility in comments, while on-site user registration was not a significant predictor. So, toxic disinhibition becomes less likely the more a user is required to be identifiable, especially to other commenters.

It also seems that a policy of prohibiting anonymity discourages user engagement, in general: Stories on news websites that prohibit anonymous usernames exhibit less comments, overall (Ksiazek, 2018). While pre-moderation of comments also predicted less comments in that study, that policy necessarily reduces the number of comments by blocking, censoring, or otherwise filtering comments before they are posted. Alternatively, prohibiting anonymity still puts the decision to comment in the hands of users, and it appears that users are less likely to comment on news websites where they are required to be publicly identifiable. Supporting this finding, Fredheim et al. (2015) analyzed a shift in HuffPost's policy regarding anonymity (from allowing anonymity to requiring third-party social media identities) and found reduced comment participation after users' identities became more recognizable.

In sum, the jury is still out on the concrete impact of anonymity policies; while some news organizations explicitly prohibit anonymous comments in an effort to improve the quality of user comments, others may choose to allow anonymity to encourage overall user engagement. Alternatively, organizations might opt for more indirect anonymity policies (on-site and/or third-party user registration) that seem to predict both more comments and reduced hostility (see Chapters 3 and 5). In the next chapter, we offer a more in-depth and comprehensive discussion of organizational commenting policies.

References

Adams, C. (2018). They go for gender first. *Journalism Practice, 12*(7), 850–869. doi: 10.1080/17512786.2017.1350115

Buckels, E. E., Trapnell, P. D., & Paulhus, D. L. (2014). Trolls just want to have fun. *Personality and Individual Differences, 67*, 97–102. doi:10.1016/j.paid.2014.01.016

Cho, D., & Kwon, K. H. (2015). The impacts of identity verification and disclosure of social cues on flaming in online user comments. *Computers in Human Behavior, 51*, 363–372. doi: 10.1016/j.chb.2015.04.046

Diakopoulos, N., & Naaman, M. (2011). Towards quality discourse in online news comments. *Proceedings of CSCW 2011* (pp. 133–142). March 19–23, Hangzhou, China. doi: 10.1145/1958824.1958844

Fredheim, R., Moore, A., & Naughton, J. (2015). Anonymity and online commenting: The broken windows effect and the end of drive-by commenting. *Proceedings of the ACM Web Science Conference.* June 28–July 1, Oxford, UK, doi: 10.1145/2786451.2786459

Joinson, A. N. (2007). Disinhibition and the Internet. In J. Gackenbach (Ed.), *Psychology and the Internet. Intrapersonal, interpersonal, and transpersonal implications* (2nd ed., pp. 75–92). San Diego: Academic Press.

Kang, R., Brown, S., & Kiesler, S. (2013). Why do people seek anonymity on the internet?: Informing policy and design. *Proceedings of the SIGCHI Conference on Human Factors in Computing Systems* (pp. 2657–2666). April 27–May 2, Paris, France. doi: 10.1145/2470654.2481368

Ksiazek, T. B. (2015). Civil interactivity: How news organizations' commenting policies explain civility and hostility in user comments. *Journal of Broadcasting & Electronic Media, 59*(4), 556–573. doi: 10.1080/08838151.2015.1093487

Ksiazek, T. B. (2018). Commenting on the news: Explaining the degree and quality of user comments on news websites. *Journalism Studies, 19*(5), 650–673. doi: 10.1080/1461670X.2016.1209977

Neurauter-Kessels, M. (2011). Im/polite reader responses on British online news sites. *Journal of Politeness Research, 7*(2), 187–214. doi:10.1515/jplr.2011.010

Nielsen, C. E. (2012). Newspaper journalists support online comments. *Newspaper Research Journal, 33*(1), 86–100. doi: 10.1177/073953291203300107

Rabab'ah, G., & Alali, N. (2020). Impoliteness in reader comments on the Al-Jazeera Channel news website. *Journal of Politeness Research, 16*(1), 1–43. doi: 10.1515/pr-2017-0028

Reader, B. (2015). *Audience feedback in the news media.* New York: Routledge.

Reich, Z. (2011). User comments. The transformation of participatory space. In J. B. Singer, A. Hermida, D. Domingo, A. Heinonen, S. Paulussen, T. Quandt, … (Eds.), *Participatory journalism. Guarding open gates at online newspapers* (pp. 96–117). Sussex: Wiley-Blackwell.

Santana, A. D. (2014). Virtuous or vitriolic. The effect of anonymity on civility in online newspaper reader comment boards. *Journalism Practice, 8*(1), 18–33. doi: 10.1080/17512786.2013.813194

Santana, A. D. (2019). Toward quality discourse: Measuring the effect of user identity in commenting forums. *Newspaper Research Journal, 40*(4), 467–486. doi: 10.1177/0739532919873089

Shanahan, M. K. (2018). *Journalism, online comments, and the future of public discourse.* New York: Routledge.

Springer, N. (2014). *Beschmutzte Öffentlichkeit? Warum Menschen die Kommentarfunktion auf Online-Nachrichtenseiten als öffentliche Toilettenwand benutzen, warum Besucher ihre Hinterlassenschaften trotzdem lesen, und wie die Wände im Anschluss aussehen*. Berlin: LIT Verlag Münster.

Suler, J. (2004). The online disinhibition effect. *Cyberpsychology & Behavior, 7*(3), 321–326. doi: 10.1089/1094931041291295

Suler, J. (2005). The online disinhibition effect. *International Journal of Applied Psychoanalytic Studies, 2*(2), 184–188. doi: 10.1002/aps.42

Wu, T. Y., & Atkin, D. (2017). Online news discussions: Exploring the role of user personality and motivations for posting comments on news. *Journalism & Mass Communication Quarterly, 94*(1), 61–80. doi: 10.1177/1077699016655754

5 Managing and improving user comments

News organizations, users, algorithms, and even artificial intelligence in the form of machine learning all play a role in managing user commentary. The current chapter begins by outlining organizational perspectives on commenting and the relevant commenting policies put in place by news organizations to manage user comments. We review empirical analysis to offer insights into which organizational commenting policies encourage more engagement (volume of comments) and better quality comments (i.e., more civil/less hostile) (Ksiazek, 2015, 2018). In a critical reflection that follows, we will shed light on the moderators' gatekeeping role and how this implemented power structure can affect the flow and content of user discussions. Given the widespread attention and varied implementation of comment moderation strategies, we devote a substantial portion of this chapter to the ways in which both organizations and users, themselves, moderate these discussion spaces. Finally, we conclude with a discussion of the current state of automation in comment moderation (i.e., artificial intelligence/machine learning).

Organizational perspectives and commenting policies: engaging users and encouraging more productive user commentary

News organizations typically have specific policies governing their comment sections. For the most part, these are designed to encourage user engagement through civil, productive interactions among users. In particular, existing empirical research suggests that policies regarding user registration, prohibiting anonymity, pre-/post-moderation, and reputation management may be effective strategies for promoting more user engagement and more civil discussion (see Table 5.1).

Table 5.1 Organizational commenting policies as predictors of user engagement (number of comments) and civility/hostility in comments

	More	*Less*

Number of comments	• User registration
	  • on-site (pseudonymous)
	  • third-party (publicly identifiable social cues)
	• Post-moderation
	• Reputation management
	• Private messaging
	• Journalist participation
		• Pre-moderation
		• Prohibiting anonymity

Civility	• Pre-moderation • Post-moderation • Reputation management	• Prohibiting anonymity
Hostility	• Private messaging	• User registration • third-party (publicly identifiable social cues) • Pre-moderation • Prohibiting anonymity • Journalist participation

Summary of results from Ksiazek's (2015, 2018) analysis of 333,605 user comments across 1379 news stories from 20 US/UK news websites.

The empirical findings presented below are drawn primarily from Ksiazek's (2015, 2018) research. In addition to the methodological description presented in Chapter 3, the following explains how each organizational commenting policy was coded:

- *on-site user registration*—coded "yes" when a news site required a user to create login credentials and a profile prior to posting a comment;
- *third-party user registration*—coded "yes" when users could log in with third-party credentials (e.g., Facebook, Twitter, Yahoo, or Google username and password);
- *prohibiting anonymity*—websites that explicitly prohibited anonymous comments were coded "yes";
- *pre-moderation*—coded "yes" when an organization screened comments prior to appearing on the site;
- *post-moderation*—coded "yes" when the site had a clear policy of removing comments that were deemed hostile or abusive;
- *reputation management*—coded "yes" when the commenting interface enabled users to rank or rate other commenters;

- *private messaging*—coded "yes" for sites that allowed private messaging between users;
- *journalist participation*—coded "yes" when the writer of a given story posted a comment in the discussion thread (Note: This is considered a practice or routine, rather than a formal policy).

A common organizational commenting policy involves requiring users to create an account and register their personal information with the news organization before commenting (Díaz Noci, Domingo, Masip, Lluís Micó, & Ruiz, 2010). Some predict that user registration should deter hostility (Coe, Kenski, & Rains, 2014; Ruiz et al., 2011). This panoptic logic is premised on the notion that hostility is discouraged by a user's awareness that their comments are connected to personally identifiable information—in essence, reflecting the impact of social control (i.e., peer pressure), or possibly a more top-down surveillance effect.

In a recent study, Ksiazek (2015) found 19 out of 20 news organizations required some form of registration in order to post a comment, although they varied in terms of whether they required on-site (pseudonymous identification, see Chapter 4) or third-party registration (publicly identifiable social cues, see Chapter 4), and in some cases, a user was given the choice of either. While both options were related to less hostile discussion, only third-party registration remained a significant predictor of less hostility when controlling for other policies. By requiring users to attach personal information to their user profile—especially if that information is held by a third party that distributes their comments to a broader social networking site (e.g., Facebook)—users are discouraged from posting hostile comments (Cho & Kwon, 2015; Fredheim, Moore, & Naughton, 2015). As we discuss in Chapter 4, an "online disinhibition effect" (Suler, 2004, 2005) is less likely to occur if users are required to publicly disclose social cues. Building on this, some research directly compares conversations about the news that take place on social media sites (where the presence of one's social network is readily apparent) to discussions that occur on news websites (often among people whose only common ground is their mutual interest in the news topic). For instance, Hille and Bakker (2014) compared user comments on Facebook to those on Dutch news websites and found, counter to what the above research might suggest, that both the quantity and quality (e.g., degree of elaboration) of comments were higher on news sites than on Facebook.

Some news organizations explicitly prohibit anonymity to encourage more civil discussion (e.g., in published commenting guidelines or codes of conduct). Reflecting on the findings in the preceding chapter, two patterns emerge. First, prohibiting anonymity reduces hostile discussion (Ksiazek, 2018). When commenters are accountable and identifiable, they seem to contribute in more productive ways. However, it also seems that a policy of prohibiting anonymity discourages user engagement, in general—stories on sites that prohibit anonymous usernames exhibit less comments, overall, than those on sites that allow anonymity (Fredheim et al., 2015; Ksiazek, 2018). And prohibiting anonymity appears to suppress the degree of civil language embodied in comment threads (i.e., terms signifying positive emotion, insight, and assent) (Ksiazek, 2018), although Santana (2019) found non-anonymous comments were more civil than anonymous comments.

Many news organizations also employ moderation tactics to limit the degree of hostility in comments. However, there is a lack of consensus on the most effective moderation strategy. Braun and Gillespie (2011) summarized the perspective of news organizations this way, "some form of comment moderation is both deeply necessary and unavoidably messy" (p. 389). Some organizations employ pre-moderation (i.e., screening comments before they appear on the site), some use post-moderation (e.g., active reviewing or retroactively removing comments that are flagged or reported as hostile), and others use a combination of both. Crawford and Gillespie (2016) highlight the widespread adoption of flagging (or post-moderation), calling the practice a "ubiquitous mechanism of governance" on social platforms (p. 411).

While it is common to conceptualize moderation in terms of pre- and post-moderation strategies, the organizations in Ksiazek's research (2015, 2018) varied in their specific approach to each policy. For example, some only pre-moderate during the initial stage for new users, while others pre-moderate with algorithms. Some engage in active post-moderation with human teams, while others only remove comments that are reported hostile (a more reactive approach). Overall, both pre-moderation and post-moderation of comments were found to be significant predictors of more civil and/or less hostile discussion. In terms of the general engagement benefit, pre-moderation necessarily reduces the overall number of comments, while the policy of post-moderation is positively related to more user comments posted to a news site. We offer an in-depth discussion of comment moderation, and recent developments to automate this process, later in this chapter.

In addition to relying on users to report or flag hostile comments, many organizations also implement reputation management systems to create a "reputation economy," where an individual's social capital is measured in terms of likes, votes, badges, and other positive indicators of their status as contributors (Braun, 2015, p. 34). In his recent study of MSNBC.com, and specifically the affiliated commenting platform *NewsVine*, Braun (2015) highlighted the use of a voting mechanism and other reputation indicators to strategically empower the community of commenters to police their own discussions by "incentiviz(ing) pro-social behavior" (p. 32). Computer science researchers have long shown that enabling an online community to manage themselves can be a powerful form of oversight (e.g., Cosley, Frankowski, Kiesler, Terveen, & Riedl, 2005).

Ksiazek's (2015, 2018) research indicates this policy is an effective predictor of both more comments and better quality conversations. The use of reputation management systems relies on crowdsourced policing of discussion platforms. In essence, news organizations are providing a way for users to hold each other accountable. The logic rests on the assumption that if a user posts hostile comments, other users will punish that user with lower reputation scores. Similarly, the logic assumes that civil commenters engaged in productive dialogue through thoughtful, informed comments will be rewarded with higher reputation scores. These reputation indicators range from virtual badges given out as rewards for certain qualities or behaviors, numerical scores, fan counts, like counts, and other comparable measures. It appears that the existence of a "reputation economy" (Braun, 2015) has a positive influence on the quality of user comments.

Ksiazek (2015, 2018) explored one final organizational commenting policy in his analysis: enabling private messaging. Many organizations in that sample offered the option for users to privately contact and send messages to other users, off-thread. The assumption was that users may be less likely to publicly post hostile comments if other commenters were able to contact them privately. That hypothesis was not supported; while the policy of providing a mechanism for private interactions between users predicted more user engagement, in terms of number of comments, that policy also predicted more hostility in public comment threads.

As we see from this review, research has explored the implementation of various combinations of these policies, as well as their effectiveness in promoting more engagement and more civil comments (Braun, 2015; Coe et al., 2014; Ksiazek, 2015, 2018; Ruiz et al., 2011; Santana, 2014). In terms of informing applied organizational practices, it is perhaps most useful to understand the overall set of policies with the greatest predictive power for both engagement and civil discussion. As Weber (2014) notes, "to realize the potential for deliberation in these public forums, the challenge is to keep the hurdles to participation low and at the same time to implement a comment management strategy that facilitates quality discourse" (p. 954).

When we account for these policies collectively, and control for other explanatory variables (story topic, use of sources, journalist participation), research finds that user registration, post-moderation, reputation management, and enabling private messaging among commenters all predicted more comments, while pre-moderation and prohibiting anonymity discouraged commenting. In terms of quality, third-party user registration, pre-moderation, post-moderation, and reputation management predicted better quality comments (i.e., more civil and/or less hostile), while the policy of prohibiting anonymity appears to reduce hostility, but also the degree of civil terms in user commentary.

Journalist participation in comment threads, while not particularly common (see Chapter 3) or considered a formal organizational policy, does positively predict more comments and less hostility (Ksiazek, 2018). From an organizational comment management perspective, this practice is relevant here because these findings suggest that formalizing or at least normalizing an expectation that journalists participate in comment threads seems to impact both overall user engagement and the relative discursive quality of user commentary.

Disruptive comment moderation: moderators as gatekeepers

Research indicates that journalists and news organizations see a need to improve the quality of user comments (e.g., Goodman, 2013; Nielsen, 2012; Santana, 2011) and that journalists and their organizations should be responsible for encouraging more civil discussion. That responsibility suggests that journalists, even in comment threads that would seemingly empower users, still embrace a traditional gatekeeping role (Wolfgang, 2018). That role is perhaps no more apparent than in the comment moderation process.

Edwards (2002) outlined a conceptual framework for the functional roles of online discussion moderators. These include: (1) the *strategic function*, "to establish the boundaries of the discussion"; (2) the *conditioning function*, to create "conditions and provisions for the discussion," including the required technologies to enable online discussion and soliciting participants; and (3) the *process function*, to manage the discussion by setting goals and agendas, encouraging participation, and "setting and maintaining the rules of the game" (pp. 6–7). In all of these functional roles, online discussion moderators establish their gatekeeping status.

When news organizations moderate comments, they are necessarily enacting a power structure that privileges the organization and its journalists over users. In a survey by the World Association of Newspapers (Goodman, 2013) of 104 news organizations from 63 countries, there was "general consensus that…it is up to the publication to determine the kind of conversation it wants to host" (p. 7). In a particularly illustrative quote, *Die Zeit* (Germany) suggested, "It's absolutely up to you as a newsroom to control what sort of comments you want to have" (p. 8). Stroud, Alizor and Lang (2016) found that 61% of US news organizations employ staff specifically to moderate user comments. In Wolfgang's (2018) ethnography of comment moderation inside a US news organization, he observed that newsroom staff "moderated silently and without sincere interaction with commenters in order to maintain journalistic authority" (p. 27). The desire for control over comment spaces suggests that news organizations across the globe view themselves as gatekeepers of user commentary.

From the user perspective, comment moderation can disrupt free speech and the free flow of dialogue and discussion. In fact, a few organizations in Goodman's (2013) survey adopted a more hands-off approach, suggesting that comment spaces should be left to users (e.g., *The Straits Times*, Singapore; *The Nation*, Kenya). Even among those who adopted moderation policies, many felt they were not limiting free speech since users are free to express themselves elsewhere online. Moreover, many felt that moderation was necessary to ensure healthy, civil interactions. For instance, *El Mercurio* (Chile) said, "We only block comments when they are offensive, we're not limiting freedom of expression, we are protecting people from offensive content" (Goodman, 2013, p. 56).

As an alternative to controlling user comments through moderation, some organizations have gone to the extreme of suspending or removing their commentary feature altogether. In the analysis of published statements on comment removal (see Chapters 1 and 6), it was clear that these organizations viewed user commentary as sufficiently disruptive to their operation as to warrant their removal. However, in many cases, these organizations cited the opportunity for users to express their opinions on social media platforms, much like the organizations in Goodman's (2013) study cited these opportunities when rationalizing how their moderation practices did not limit free speech. Still, and perhaps unsurprisingly, Liu and McLeod (2019) found that users view comment removal as disruptive, with active commenters more likely to oppose removal than non-users of commentary features.

Comment moderation in practice

For the management of user discussions in commenting spaces, outlets usually interpret the "moderation" role as policing and banning problematic contributions. However, outlets with more participatory mindsets, as well as the necessary resources, can get inspiration about this role from academic literature on "group discussions," where the moderator has a relevant share in safeguarding a discussion's success, that is, facilitating a productive, respectful conversation and rich interaction between the participants (Grønkjær, Curtis, de Crespigny, & Delmar, 2011, p. 22; Parker & Tritter, 2006, p. 26). While a moderator should avoid interfering if a discussion is self-containing, stimulating and initiating engagement, addressing all participants is encouraged if conversations come to a halt (Bohnsack, 2004, p. 219). Thoughtful intervention can be applied when discussions drift or derail, and also ensure that all participants have a chance to be heard (Grønkjær et al., 2011, pp. 24–26). In specific research settings, moderators even serve to summarize discussions (Parker & Tritter, 2006, p. 26). With these two role conceptions in mind, scholarly work on comment moderation in practice identifies the following two general approaches to news outlets' comment moderation (e.g., Springer, 2014):

- *Policing.* Moderation can focus on identifying and deleting legally problematic content or content that violates codes of conduct which are usually published on their sites (Ziegele & Jost, 2016, classify this form of moderation as "content moderation"). Here, moderation remains reactive or hidden "behind the scenes," since it does not (publicly) mediate between editorial staff and users, or between users (see also Wolfgang, 2018). In the worst case, the post is removed (post-moderation) or never published (pre-moderation), and the user does not get informed about this intervention and never learns why. In the best case, moderators inform a commenter about reasons for why a comment had not been published; in order to also inform others, such banning can be communicated publicly (e.g., instead of publishing the banned comment, a message can be posted that "this comment violated our code of conduct").
- *Engaging.* Moderators can also be present and active in comment threads (Ziegele and Jost (2016) classify this as "interactive moderation"). Their engagement can be supportive/rewarding or regulative/sanctioning (Ziegele & Jost, 2016; Ziegele, Jost, Bormann, & Heinbach, 2018). Supportive moderators can

> introduce a topic, provide (additional) information, answer questions or ask users to elaborate interesting claims. Taking on a more general role of "community managers," moderators can also mediate between editors and users or express their and the newsroom's appreciation. In a regulative role, they can ask users to remain on the topic, remain respectful, or mediate conflicts between them. Research on engaging moderation styles suggest that this form of engagement—especially if representing journalists personally—can positively impact readers' willingness to participate (Ziegele & Jost, 2016), decrease incivility, and result in a greater provision of evidence in comments (Stroud, Scacco, Muddiman, & Curry, 2015; see also Ziegele et al., 2018). However, news outlets are advised to engage in an appropriate way: Regulative (patronizing) moderation can lead to more uncivil user reactions (Ziegele et al., 2018). In addition, experimental research shows that while a sarcastic moderation style might be more entertaining to read, it can negatively affect credibility assessments, thereby quality perceptions, and thus reduce the willingness to participate (Ziegele & Jost, 2016). A factual moderation of uncivil user comments, however, conveys a deliberative discussion atmosphere, which is appealing to users and thus stimulates the participants' willingness to engage (ibid.).

Comment moderation can also be supported by users, which is a mode that Ziegele and Jost (2016) call "collaborative moderation." Here, peers are exerting social control in order to shape and enforce discussion norms in comment spaces. Usually, users are provided features to flag or report, sometimes even to dislike comments if they are deemed problematic (like-buttons to indicate approval or agreement are also common). Comments "with enough flags can then be automatically removed from the site or sent to a moderator for review" (p. 5). Moreover, users can also engage by replying to other comments they disagree with or find triggering (or praise constructive contributions). More organized acts of counter-speech or "corrective action" (Ziegele, Naab, & Jost, 2019) had already been touched upon in Chapter 3.

Research suggests that informing readers about commenting policies/codes of conduct, intervention options, and encouragement to do so increases their likelihood to report problematic content (Naab, Kalch, & Meitz, 2018). Readers will most likely only engage in one, or sometimes two, forms of sanctioning action (disliking, flagging, or replying), and given the lower thresholds and higher "costs" in regard to time and effort, users are more likely to engage in disliking and flagging than replying (Kalch & Naab, 2017). Persons with a more positive attitude toward a criticized group are especially likely to report comments impolitely attacking this group (p. 407). These authors found that in general, impoliteness, not incivility, influenced whether intervening flagging and replying was triggered, a finding that challenges “the reliability of user engagement” in comment moderation efforts (Kalch & Naab, 2017, p. 410), at least, if comment moderation solely relies on users spotting problematic content. Sanctioning user actions were also found to depend “on characteristics of the course of the discussion” (Naab et al., 2018, p. 789): Other commenters’ agreement with an uncivil and impolite comment “increases the attribution of responsibility to professional moderators that in turn increases flagging to inform moderators” (ibid.). However, flagging is “less likely if an abstract social group is attacked, in particular if a disagreeing response has already been posted” (p. 785). Reading a countering comment by another user will reduce attributed responsibility, but this reply needs to have the right amount of sanctioning potential: “a polite response does not reduce attributed responsibility, and thus flagging” (p. 789). Such a reply is probably “not perceived as an adequate reaction so that further intervention is in need” (ibid.). Research investigating who actually engages in such “bystander intervention” by reporting comments (Watson, Peng, & Lewis, 2019) suggests that (the frequency of) this form of social control is positively associated with trust in the news and an authoritarian personality, and most likely (more often) exerted by younger, White, and male readers/commenters (p. 1851). Watson and colleagues (2019) remark that such users belong to those groups of people “who already have greater social advantages, including being more encouraged to speak up in public forums” (p. 1853).

In regard to verbalized reactions (i.e., replying to other commenters), the study by Kalch and Naab (2017) suggests that impolite comments will trigger responses that criticize the language style, while polite comments will trigger comments positioned “against the expressed opinion” (p. 410). Interestingly, experiment participants with more negative attitudes toward a group criticized in a comment replied more often to the polite and uncivil version but less often to the impolite and uncivil version of this comment—thus, politeness in comments seems to be a cue signaling “valuable discussion that is worthy of further participation” (pp. 410–411). Correspondingly, participants with a more positive attitude also reacted more often upon polite and civil (yet critical) comments (p. 410). Personal characteristics and drivers to engage in (organized) “corrective actions” against uncivil comments were found to be feelings of personal responsibility, self-efficacy (a perception of being able to intervene, that is: High efficacy in comment writing) as well as the expectation of personal benefits "such as reputation and appreciation" (Ziegele et al., 2019, p. 15). Additional "collective action" driving factors were found to be the perceived "group efficacy and knowledge of the rules and structures of the movement" (p. 1).

Braun (2015) observes the increasing use of "collapsing algorithms" that effectively filter out (or "collapse") comments that reach a threshold of low user ratings. Interestingly, this practice integrates two of the organizational commenting policies that seem to have a positive impact on comment quality: automated moderation and socially driven reputation management systems, where communities of users hold each other accountable through ratings and rankings. In the following section, we delve deeper into further developments in automation in comment moderation.

Automation in comment moderation practice

The positive impact of sociable, engaging moderation will most likely be beneficial beyond improving the quality of user commentary: When participation rates increase, they lead to a higher reach and more engagement with news sites; thus, a promise for more impact and revenues. In addition, news outlets that have not (yet) decided to close down their comment sections or shift them to their social media platforms still seem to believe in the value of public debate and in potential input for editorial processes. However, engaged moderation requires a lot of resources for unsure outcomes, which is why automation becomes not only the 'latest thing' but seemingly also a 'last resort.'

In order to manage the overwhelming stream of incoming user-generated contributions, automated solutions are being intensively investigated, oftentimes in joint endeavors by the industry and the academy (e.g., Loosen et al., 2017; Schabus, Skowron, & Trapp, 2017). While profanity filters have been common for some time (see, e.g., Singer et al., 2011), the latest endeavors experiment with Artificial Intelligence, and more specifically, with machine learning, for instance to automatically detect incivility and impoliteness in user comments (e.g., Schabus et al., 2017; Stoll, Ziegele, & Quiring, 2019).[1] Computational scientists bring their expertise in automation to the table, while communication scholars possess valuable knowledge about more general usage practices and factors influencing those; in addition, the industry has important practical experiences with users' commenting behavior, comment moderation in practice, as well as the data necessary to train algorithms (e.g., the "One million posts corpus," a repository of comments posted to the Austrian "Der Standard"; or the New York Times "Community API"; see Diakopoulos, 2015; Park, Sachar, Diakopoulos, & Elmqvist, 2016; Schabus et al., 2017).

Machine learning describes the automated process of classifying (elements of) texts by means of algorithms that can be trained in supervised or unsupervised settings. Within supervised machine learning, algorithms' training requires an annotated set of comments: Like quantitative content analyses, a corpus of user posts is structurally coded according to previously defined categories (in machine learning contexts, this process is called "annotation"). The training can begin once a reliably and sufficiently large corpus of user comments is coded; the bigger this corpus, the better for the training's results. This corpus' codings reflect the 'gold standard' against which the algorithms' accuracy is tested. For the training, the corpus is split into two datasets: a training dataset (e.g., containing 80% of the cases) and a dataset for out-of-sample validation (the remaining 20%; Haim, Heinzel, Lankheit, Niagu, & Springer, 2019). Mathematically different machine learning approaches exist (e.g., Jurka, Collingwood, Boydstun, Grossman, & van Atteveldt, 2013) and have been tested for the classification of comments (e.g., Haim et al., 2019; Häring, Loosen, & Maalej, 2018; Schabus et al., 2017). The algorithms these approaches represent eventually take on the task of continuing to classify future incoming comments independently, by means of predictive models that estimate these codes based on language patterns (Stoll et al., 2019, p. 17). The performance or accuracy of these models are then assessed by "precision-," "recall-," and "f-scores": The precision-score reflects "how often a case the algorithm predicts as belonging to a class actually belongs to that class" (Jurka et al., 2013, p. 9). Conversely, recall-scores reflect the proportion of classifications in a class that "the algorithm correctly assigns to that class" (ibid.). Finally, f-scores "produce a weighted average of both precision and recall" (ibid.).

In the spirit of an engaging moderation style, the latest automation efforts not only focus on the development of classifiers for the identification of problematic commentary, but also engage in the experimentation of how to identify interesting and constructive commentary (e.g., Haim et al., 2019; Häring et al., 2018; Park et al., 2016; Schabus et al., 2017). Once such comments are identified, they can be featured prominently (e.g., the New York Times "picks"), a reward for the comments' authors that should positively impact their future commenting behavior. In addition, comments can contain interesting information for journalists or moderators to consider; an automated identification of such elements (e.g., user feedback or valuable leads for follow-up stories) makes it easier for the newsrooms to process and include this information into their daily workflows (e.g., Park et al., 2016, p. 1117; see also Häring et al., 2018). In what follows, we delve deeper into the academic discussion about how to assess and automatically detect useful comments.

While this represents only one perspective, editorial or journalistic criteria can serve as an inspiration to assess user comments and "computationally operationalize" (Diakopoulos, 2015, p. 154) relevant qualities such as their "constructiveness" (Kolhatkar & Taboada, 2017; see also Park et al., 2016). Both content-related and user-history-related criteria for automated classification are considered. Building on Diakopoulos's (2015) work, Park and colleagues (2016, p. 1118) suggest computationally operationalizing quality criteria, such as: (1) comments' relevance in regard to the article (*article relevance*) and (2) their relevance in regard to proceeding comments (*conversational relevance*), (3) their *length* in words, (4) whether they contain *personal experience* and whether they are (5) readable (*readability*), as well as (6) how often a comment had been recommended by others (*recommendation*). Regarding an individual commenter's history, useful criteria can be: (7) the average amount of comments a user posts per month (*user comment rate*), (8) the average *user comment length*, (9) the *average personal experience* score, (10) *user readability* score, and (11) *user recommendation* score across a user's commenting history as well as (12) the average rate at which a commenter's posts had been recognized as "New York Times picks" (*user picks*). Building on their work, Kolhatkar and Taboada (2017) head in a similar direction and suggest "constructiveness features" (p. 102) that are based on: (A) *length features* (e.g., the "number of sentences" and "average number of words per sentence"), (B) *named-entity features* (that take into account the number of entities named in a comment), (C) *text quality features* (a readability score and "personal experiences description score," see also Park et al., 2016), as well as (D) *argumentation features*. The latter is particularly interesting: "Argumentation features" can measure users' applications of discourse connectives, such as "therefore"; reasoning verbs, such as "cause"; modals, such as "should"; abstract nouns, such as "issue"; or stance adverbials, such as "undoubtedly" (Kolhatkar & Taboada, 2017, pp. 102–103). To detect argumentation in comments, a reference to sources can also be a helpful indicator (Haim et al., 2019; Schabus et al., 2017). Several more additions are possible and/or have already been explored: The inclusion of temporal or geographical information (e.g., Park et al., 2016), measures for comments' "novelty," "criticality," and "thoughtfulness" (ibid., p. 1123), or sentiment (e.g., Loosen et al., 2017; Schabus et al., 2017).

Personal stories seem particularly interesting for newsrooms to detect (e.g., Haim et al., 2019; Park et al., 2016; Schabus et al., 2017). Some of the users' accounts—be it personal stories, arguments or evidence provided in a comment—can be worthy of further journalistic engagement. However, given that the real person behind a commenter's nickname is most likely unknown, the verification of these user accounts is especially relevant. To identify potential, trustworthy sources, classifiers such as "user reputation" and "commenting frequency" can provide important cues (Park et al., 2016, p. 1122). In addition, some research has also explored automated identification of "meta-comments" that contain some form of feedback to the newsroom (Häring et al., 2018; see also Schabus et al., 2017). A qualitative analysis of such "meta-comments" by Häring and colleagues (2018) suggests that these contain elements that members of the newsrooms or community managers could react upon; such elements include user critique (like asking for justifications, missing information, reporting errors, and providing corrections) as well as questions (regarding an article but also the comment moderation, such as the reasoning behind the blocking of contributions). Häring and colleagues (2018) also found evidence of praising or recommending articles to other readers in meta-comments.

In the studies discussed above, the performance of these classifiers ranges from mediocre to promising, depending on the constructs' and thus the operationalizations' complexity and training-data-quality (Haim et al., 2019; Häring et al., 2018; Kolhatkar & Taboada 2017, pp. 103–104; Park et al., 2016, p. 1118; Schabus et al., 2017; Stoll et al., 2019). Thus, it is only realistic that practical solutions are based on semi-automated moderation where human moderators are supported by automation (Haim et al., 2019). Which of the identification criteria are considered helpful and acceptable lies certainly in the eye of the beholder: for instance, the use of commenters' personal data raises data privacy concerns (Haim et al., 2019). Also, shorter comments with weaker associations to an article can provide unexpected perspectives (Park et al., 2016). Park and colleagues (2016) therefore suggest that "each score must be used carefully while critically considering limitations" (p. 1123).

Eventually, these automation endeavors should result in solutions that are flexible, adjustable, and tailored to serve moderators and journalists in their respective daily routines, tasks, and workflows. This is why solutions are often brainstormed, discussed, and validated in interviews or discussions with moderators and journalists (e.g., Haim et al., 2019; Loosen et al., 2017; Park et al., 2016). Also, 'front end' users should be considered, that is, how these solutions can support commenters' and readers' user experiences, increasing their view time and engagement with the respective site (e.g., Park et al., 2016). Accordingly, AI supported moderation tools applied in the industry, as developed by the Coral Project, allow newsrooms to give feedback to commenters, for instance, but also make it possible for commenters to identify journalists in discussions or to "[m]ute annoying voices" (Coral Project, n.d.).

In summary, automation can help to detect valuable contributions that otherwise might vanish or go unnoticed in the stream of incoming user postings. These contributions can be prominently featured to illustrate ideal communication norms in comment sections (Haim et al., 2019) and/or inform the news production process. Such a treatment should serve as positive, rewarding feedback to commenters, resulting in their encouragement and empowerment. The hope is that journalists can see more potential in users' contributions and that they engage in a more collaborative process with these contributors, perhaps reaching the potential described in the scholarly concept of "participatory journalism" (see Chapter 1). Moderation approaches as outlined in this chapter promise a more equal relationship between users and journalists, rather than a top-down, banning approach or journalistic ignorance.

Note

1 The industry also engages in automating the measurement of "toxicity" in online communication, for instance, with the Perspective API developed by Jigsaw and Google's "Counter Abuse Technology team." As described on their website, the "API uses machine learning models to score the perceived impact a comment might have on a conversation. Developers and publishers can use this score to give real-time feedback to commenters or help moderators do their job, or allow readers to more easily find relevant information.... Our first model identifies whether a comment could be perceived as 'toxic' to a discussion" (https://www.perspectiveapi.com/#/home).

References

Bohnsack, R. (2004). Group discussion and focus groups. In U. Flick, E. von Kardoff, & I. Steinke (Eds.), *A companion to qualitative research* (pp. 214–221). London, Thousand Oaks, New Delhi: Sage.

Braun, J. A. (2015). News programs: Designing MSNBC.com's online interfaces. *Journalism, 16*(1), 27–43. doi: 10.1177/1464884914545730

Braun, J., & Gillespie, T. (2011). Hosting the public discourse, hosting the public: When online news and social media converge. *Journalism Practice, 5*(4), 383–398. doi: 10.1080/17512786.2011.557560

Cho, D., & Kwon, K. H. (2015). The impacts of identity verification and disclosure of social cues on flaming in online user comments. *Computers in Human Behavior, 51*, 363–372. doi: 10.1016/j.chb.2015.04.046

Coe, K., Kenski, K., & Rains, S. A. (2014). Online and uncivil? Patterns and determinants of incivility in newspaper website comments. *Journal of Communication, 64*, 658–679. doi: 10.1111/jcom.12104

Coral Project (n.d.). Your community is our priority. Retrieved from https://coralproject.net/tour/

Cosley, D., Frankowski, D., Kiesler, S., Terveen, L., & Riedl, J. (2005). How oversight improves member-maintained communities. *Proceedings of CHI*, 2005 (pp. 11–20). doi: 10.1145/1054972.1054975

Crawford, K., & Gillespie, T. (2016). What is a flag for? Social media reporting tools and the vocabulary of complaint. *New Media & Society, 18*(3), 410–428. doi: 10.1177/1461444814543163

Diakopoulos, N. (2015). Picking the NYT Picks: Editorial criteria and automation in the curation of online news comments. *ISOJ Journal, 6*(1), 147–166.

Díaz Noci, J., Domingo, D., Masip, P., Lluís Micó, J., & Ruiz, C. (2010). Comments in news, democracy booster or journalistic nightmare: Assessing the quality and dynamics of citizen debates in Catalan online newspapers. *International Symposium on Online Journalism*. Austin. April 23–24.

Edwards, A. R. (2002). The moderator as an emerging democratic intermediary: The role of the moderator in Internet discussions about public issues. *Information Polity, 7*(1), 3–20. doi: 10.3233/IP-2002-0002

Fredheim, R., Moore, A., & Naughton, J. (2015). Anonymity and online commenting: The broken windows effect and the end of drive-by commenting. *Proceedings of the ACM Web Science Conference*. June 28–July 1, Oxford, UK, doi: 10.1145/2786451.2786459

Goodman, E. (2013). Online comment moderation: Emerging best practices. *World Association of Newspapers (WAN-IFRA)*. Retrieved from http://www.wan-ifra.org/reports/2013/10/04/online-comment-moderation-emerging-best-practices

Grønkjær, M., Curtis, T., de Crespigny, C., & Delmar, C. (2011). Analysing group interaction in focus group research: Impact on content and the role of the moderator. *Qualitative Studies, 2*(1), 16–30doi: 10.7146/qs.v2i1.4273

Haim, M., Heinzel, I., Lankheit, S., Niagu, A. M., & Springer, N. (2019, May). *Identifying the good and the bad: Using machine learning to moderate user commentary on news*. Paper presentation at the annual International Communication Association (ICA) conference, Washington, DC.

Häring, M., Loosen, W., & Maalej, W. (2018). Who is addressed in this comment?: Automatically classifying meta-comments in news comments. *Proceedings of the ACM on Human-Computer Interaction, 2*(CSCW), 67. doi: 10.1145/3274336

Hille, S., & Bakker, P. (2014). Engaging the social news user: Comments on news sites and Facebook. *Journalism Practice, 8*(5), 563–572. doi: 10.1080/17512786.2014.899758

Jurka, T. P., Collingwood, L., Boydstun, A. E., Grossman, E., & van Atteveldt, W. (2013). RTextTools: A supervised learning package for text classification. *The R Journal, 5*(1), 6–12.

Kalch, A., & Naab, T. K. (2017). Replying, disliking, flagging: How users engage with uncivil and impolite comments on news sites. *Studies in Communication and Media, 6*(4), 395–419. doi: 10.5771/2192-4007-2017-4-395

Kolhatkar, V., & Taboada, M. (2017). Using New York Times Picks to identify constructive comments. *Proceedings of the 2017 EMNLP Workshop: Natural Language Processing meets Journalism* (pp. 100–105). September, Copenhagen, Denmark. doi: 10.18653/v1/W17-42

Ksiazek, T. B. (2015). Civil interactivity: How news organizations' commenting policies explain civility and hostility in user comments. *Journal of Broadcasting & Electronic Media, 59*(4), 556–573. doi: 10.1080/08838151.2015.1093487

Ksiazek, T. B. (2018). Commenting on the news: Explaining the degree and quality of user comments on news websites. *Journalism Studies, 19*(5), 650–673. doi: 10.1080/1461670X.2016.1209977

Liu, J., & McLeod, D. M. (2019). Pathways to news commenting and the removal of the comment system on news websites. *Journalism*. Advanced Online Publication. doi: 10.1177/1464884919849954

Loosen, W., Häring, M., Kurtanović, Z., Merten, L., Reimer, J., van Roessel, L., & Maalej, W. (2017). Making sense of user comments: Identifying journalists' requirements for a comment analysis framework. *Studies in Communication and Media, 6*(4), 333–364. doi: 10.5771/2192-4007-2017-4-333

Naab, T. K., Kalch, A., & Meitz, T. G. (2018). Flagging uncivil user comments: Effects of intervention information, type of victim, and response comments on bystander behavior. *New Media & Society, 20*(2), 777–795. doi: 10.1177/1461444816670923

Nielsen, C. E. (2012). Newspaper journalists support online comments. *Newspaper Research Journal, 33*(1), 86–100. doi: 10.1177/073953291203300107

Park, D., Sachar, S., Diakopoulos, N., & Elmqvist, N. (2016, May). Supporting comment moderators in identifying high quality online news comments. *Proceedings of the 2016 CHI Conference on Human Factors in Computing Systems* (pp. 1114–1125). May 7–12, San Jose, California. ACM. doi: 10.1145/2858036.2858389

Parker, A., & Tritter, J. (2006). Focus group method and methodology: Current practice and recent debate. *International Journal of Research & Method in Education, 29*(1), 23–37. doi: 10.1080/01406720500537304

Ruiz, C., Domingo, D., Micó, J. L., Díaz-Noci, J., Meso, K., & Masip, P. (2011). Public sphere 2.0? The democratic qualities of citizen debates in online newspapers. *The International Journal of Press/Politics, 16*(4), 463–487. doi: 10.1177/1940161211415849

Santana, A. D. (2011). Online readers' comments represent new opinion pipeline. *Newspaper Research Journal, 32*(3), 66–81. doi: 10.1177/073953291103200306

Santana, A. D. (2014). Virtuous or vitriolic. The effect of anonymity on civility in online newspaper reader comment boards. *Journalism Practice, 8*(1), 18–33. doi: 10.1080/17512786.2013.813194

Santana, A. D. (2019). Toward quality discourse: Measuring the effect of user identity in commenting forums. *Newspaper Research Journal, 40*(4), 467–486. doi: 10.1177/0739532919873089

Schabus, D., Skowron, M., & Trapp, M. (2017). One million posts: A data set of German online discussions. *Proceedings of the 40th International ACM SIGIR Conference on Research and Development in Information Retrieval (SIGIR)* (pp. 1241–1244). August 7–11, Tokyo, Japan. doi: 10.1145/3077136.3080711

Shanahan, M. K. (2018). *Journalism, online comments, and the future of public discourse.* New York: Routledge.

Singer, J. B., Hermida, A., Domingo, D., Heinonen, A., Paulussen, S., Quandt, T., …, Vujnovic, M. (Eds.). (2011). *Participatory journalism. Guarding open gates at online newspapers.* Sussex: Wiley-Blackwell.

Springer, N. (2014). *Beschmutzte Öffentlichkeit? Warum Menschen die Kommentarfunktion auf Online-Nachrichtenseiten als öffentliche Toilettenwand benutzen, warum Besucher ihre Hinterlassenschaften trotzdem lesen, und wie die Wände im Anschluss aussehen.* Berlin: LIT Verlag Münster.

Stoll, A., Ziegele, M., & Quiring, O. (2019). *Detecting incivility and impoliteness in online discussions. Classification approaches for German user comments.* Retrieved from https://osf.io/preprints/socarxiv/a47ch/

Stroud, N. J., Alizor, A., & Lang, C. (2016). Survey of news editors and directors. *Engaging News Project. Annette Strauss Institute for Civic Life*, University of Texas at Austin. Retrieved from https://mediaengagement.org/wp-content/uploads/2016/08/ENP-Survey-of-News-Editors-and-Directors.pdf

Stroud, N. J., Scacco, J. M., Muddiman, A., & Curry, A. L. (2015). Changing deliberative norms on news organizations' Facebook sites. *Journal of Computer-Mediated Communication, 20*(2), 188–203. doi: 10.1111/jcc4.12104

Suler, J. (2004). The online disinhibition effect. *Cyberpsychology & Behavior, 7*(3), 321–326. doi: 10.1089/1094931041291295

Suler, J. (2005). The online disinhibition effect. *International Journal of Applied Psychoanalytic Studies, 2*(2), 184–188. doi: 10.1002/aps.42

Watson, B. R., Peng, Z., & Lewis, S. C., (2019). Who will intervene to save news comments? Deviance and social control in communities of news commenters. *New Media and Society*, online first. doi: 10.1177/1461444819828328

Weber, P. (2014). Discussions in the comments section: Factors influencing participation and interactivity in online newspapers' reader comments. *New Media & Society, 16*(6), 941–957. doi: 10.1177/1461444813495165

Wolfgang, J. D. (2018). Cleaning up the "fetid swamp:" Examining how journalists construct policies and practices for moderating comments. *Digital Journalism, 6*(1), 21–40. doi: 10.1080/21670811.2017.1343090

Ziegele, M., & Jost, P. B. (2016). Not funny? The effects of factual versus sarcastic journalistic responses to uncivil user comments. *Communication Research.* Advance online publication. doi: 10.1177/0093650216671854

Ziegele, M., Jost, P., Bormann, M., & Heinbach, D. (2018). Journalistic counter-voices in comment sections: Patterns, determinants, and potential consequences of interactive moderation of uncivil user comments. *Studies in Communication and Media, 7*(4), 525–554. doi: 10.5771/2192–4007-2018-4–525

Ziegele, M., Naab, T. K., & Jost, P. (2019). Lonely together? Identifying the determinants of collective corrective action against uncivil comments. *New Media & Society.* Advance online publication. doi: 1461444819870130

6 Where do we go from here?

In recent years, comments have been praised; analyzed; criticized; and, as a result, sometimes banned from news sites. The quality of user comments seems to be the most pressing issue, and we see two possible paths forward for news organizations: either shut comments off entirely (and relegate users to social media platforms) or take greater ownership through improved comment moderation. The reality is that media outlets introduced commenting spaces to build user engagement and generate revenues, and investing serious resources into curating public discussions was never really a top priority. Since organizations did not take great interest in what happened "below the line," comment threads tended to become shout boxes, with concerns about incivility abound.

This final chapter begins by returning to our focus on user commentary as disruptive engagement, examining the debate about whether the field of digital journalism should abandon comments (as some organizations have done) or find ways to encourage more productive commentary by critically assessing and reflecting on currently insufficient moderation strategies (e.g., those that are focused on policing and banning instead of being engaging and encouraging). We advocate for the latter position, returning to reflect on our discussions in the preceding chapters. In doing so, we propose an *Integrated Comment Moderation Model* that captures best practices and collaboration among user-driven moderation, organizational policies for encouraging more productive commentary, and innovations in the areas of automation in moderation.

Disruptive engagement and moderation: abandon or encourage more productive commentary?

Research suggests serious concerns in the news industry about the quality (e.g., civility) of user comments. In our analysis of recent public statements from news organizations about their rationale for removing comments, we found extensive references to incivility as a reason for removing commentary functions. Echoing these concerns, Wolfgang (2018) found that "Journalists disliked moderating conversations and spoke about contributions derisively, therefore establishing low expectations of the commenter…[and] describing the forums using terms like 'cesspool' or 'fetid swamp'" (p. 27). Meltzer's (2015) analysis of more general industry discourse about user comments also found widespread concern among news professionals about incivility in comments. Similarly, in Goodman's (2013) study for The World Association of Newspapers of 100+ news organizations across 63 countries, staff expressed concerns about the general quality of these discussions, along with the resources necessary to curate more productive discussion spaces. Despite these critiques about various forms of "dark participation" (Quandt, 2018), the corresponding concern for encouraging more productive user commentary is noteworthy. Others have also found evidence that journalists and news organizations have a desire to improve the quality of user comments (e.g., Nielsen, 2012; Santana, 2011).

Yet, in recent years, we've seen a growing number of news organizations abandon their commentary features, rather than tackle the perceived problem head-on. Here, we return to our comment removal analysis from Chapter 1 to inform the debate between abandoning user commentary or encouraging more productive commentary.

To begin, let us say a bit more about the empirical method used in this analysis. The first stage in the analytical process involved identifying a set of news organizations that recently made the decision to remove comment functions housed on their online platforms. This purposive sample was collected in April and May of 2019 by a combination of the following procedures. First, we combed through various lists of top news organizations compiled by the Nieman Journalism Lab and the Pew Research Center. Second, we searched the following major trade publications and associations for articles about news organizations removing their commentary features: *American Journalism Review*, *Association for Education in Journalism and Mass Communication*, *Broadcasting & Cable*, *Columbia Journalism Review*, *Editor & Publisher*, *Journalist's Resource*, *MediaPost*, *Media Week*, *Multichannel News*, *National Association of Broadcasters*, *Radio Ink*, *Society of Professional Journalists*, and *TV NewsCheck*. Third, we conducted a LexisNexis search for articles about commentary removal. We used the search term *remov* comment* news* to search all lists, organizations, publications, and databases to identify articles mentioning comment removal.[1]

After identifying news outlets that had moved or removed commenting functions from their websites, published statements regarding this decision were collected. Though many news organizations released statements describing the decision to remove commenting capabilities from their web platforms, many others made no effort to inform their readers as to why commenting was no longer available. Out of the 28 national and local news outlets identified as having removed their commenting functions from their websites, only 15 were found to have published statements or articles regarding the change, with an additional five included in the sample based on the grounds that their commenting policy referenced the removal or limiting of commenting functions. During the analysis, depending on the query involved, these five outliers were included or removed from the dataset in order to gain a more holistic sense of the framing of news organizations' decision to end, or severely curtail, commenting functions for their online articles (see Table 6.1 for a list of the news organizations included in the comment removal analysis).

Upon identifying the 20 relevant statements and policies, the text of each was uploaded into the NVivo software and identified within by news organization, date, title, and associated author(s) whenever available. The codebook was developed iteratively throughout the analysis phase and was continually refined and revised in order to fully reflect the language, themes, and common characteristics of the statements and policies in question. Key parent nodes included references to good commenting practices, bad commenting practices, and moderation techniques or explanations. These nodes were cross-coded to capture specific language used to describe comment function removal, civil and uncivil discussion, and news organizations' ideal community of online readership. Some of these associations were

Table 6.1 News organizations included in comment removal analysis

• BBC	• Popular Science	• The Mic
• CNN	• Recode	• The Verge
• Hartford Courant	• Reuters	• The Week
• Huffington Post	• The Atlantic	• USA Today
• New York Times	• The Daily Dot	• Vice
• Newsday	• The Daily Beast	• Washington Post
• NPR	• The Guardian	

Outlets that removed comment feature, but had no published statement available for inclusion in the analysis: Atlanta Journal Constitution; Bloomberg; Buffalo News; Chicago Sun Times; Chicago Tribune; MSNBC; New York Daily News; The Washington Inquirer.

veiled or implicit, while other writers condemned specific behaviors, ideologies, or motivations.

The analysis draws on both quantitative content analysis (text mining; keyword frequency analysis) and manual qualitative analysis using grounded theory (Strauss & Corbin, 1990) to identify themes in the organizational reasoning for removing comments. Reflecting a growing trend in the discipline, this research design combines both manual and automated content analysis. As Lewis, Zamith and Hermida (2013) argue, "hybrid combinations of computational and manual approaches can preserve the strengths of traditional content analysis, with its systematic rigor and contextual awareness, while maximizing the large-scale capacity of Big Data and the efficiencies of computational methods" (p. 47).

Published statements on comment removal tended to follow a similar arc. Many began with a description of the toll that comment section moderation and poor quality commenting practices (i.e., incivility) had taken on the organization and its writers (see Chapter 5). Frequently noted in these descriptions was the trend toward comment removal in the wider landscape of online news websites. The statements often moved on to a discussion of other ways that readers are able to provide commentary on news articles, with an emphasis on social media platforms as alternative outlets for the continuation of constructive conversation. Another frequently appearing theme emphasized how organizations inherently valued their online community of readers and their honest feedback and criticism, which news outlets viewed as enhancing journalistic coverage.

Organizational rationales for removing comments ranged from concerns about incivility, to a variety of commenting effects (see Chapter 3), including: the idea that bad commenters were skewing public perception of the news stories, scientific facts, or the news organization itself; to the protection of sensitive subjects, content, and the reputation of journalists. Related to the latter concern, some organizational statements framed the reasoning for removing comment sections as a way to take a stand against readers who share prejudicial sentiments specifically directed at journalists (what the Guardian's Stephen Pritchard termed "author abuse" (Pritchard, 2016, March 26). Overall, the analysis revealed extensive references to incivility as the most common reason for removing commentary functions.

There was also an overwhelming emphasis on the shift to commenting via social media, especially focusing on Facebook and Twitter as places where user commentary already does and ought to take place. What was sometimes explicitly stated, but more often alluded to, was the sheer power of mass moderation and strict community guidelines imposed upon users by most social media platforms. In outsourcing the location of user commentary, news sites not only put a buffer between themselves and potentially vitriolic conversation, but they also free up resources that would otherwise be absorbed by the maintenance of their own comment sections (see Chapter 5).

While many organizations have removed comments site-wide, some (e.g., The Guardian, The Washington Post, and The New York Times) have banned comments on strictly news-related articles, while opinion and popular culture articles remain open to platform-hosted reader discussions. Judgments about the difference between articles that are good candidates for user commentary and those that are not is a notable exercise for news organizations and offer insight about how news organizations and journalists understand their role as gatekeepers in this context (see Chapter 5). Rather than running the risk of housing uncivil discussions by readers or spreading misinformation, these news organizations have made the executive decision that user commentary, though valuable, is better left to more frivolous, less journalistically intensive topics relegated to the culture and opinion sections.

Research suggests that commenters and comment readers oppose the trend toward shutting down comment spaces (e.g., Liu & McLeod, 2019). Rather than giving up on commenting features, as a growing number of news organizations have done, we advocate for embracing commentary for all its deliberative potential and see improved moderation practices as the best way forward. In the next section, we argue that the most effective means to that end involve an Integrated Comment Moderation Model (Figure 6.1).

Integrated Comment Moderation Model

As established in Chapter 5, comment moderation efforts can be conceptualized as a continuum with one end being "policing and banning only" and the other "active moderation in a helpful mindset" (see for instance Ziegele & Jost, 2016; Ziegele, Jost, Bormann, & Heinbach, 2018; or the work by the Center for Media Engagement at the University of Texas at Austin). Due to limited resources, most outlets practice "policing and banning only" strategies, but with such a mindset, allowing for user comments is a huge investment that does not necessarily pay back journalistically (although comments drive engagement and thus indirect revenues). This echoes concerns in Goodman's (2013) study about the resources required to properly moderate and curate productive discussions.

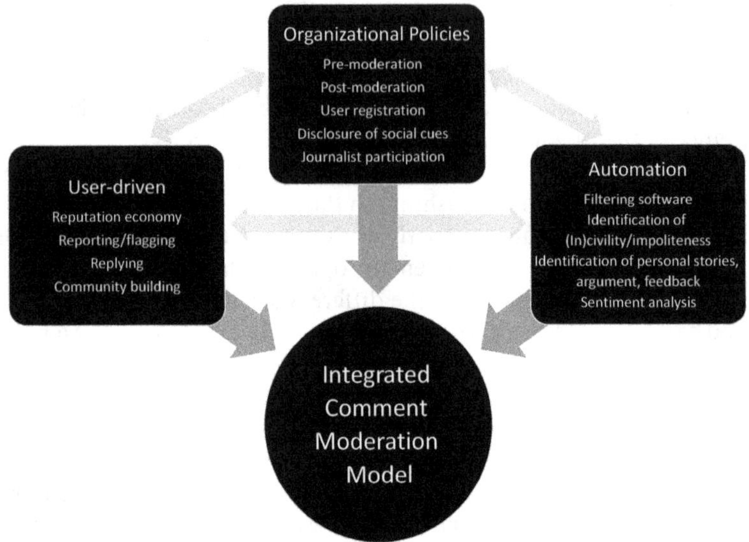

Figure 6.1 Integrated Comment Moderation Model.

Drawing on recent literature on newsrooms' engagement in user discussions, we assume that active moderation should have positive effects on the level of user participation and the civility of discussions (Ksiazek, 2015, 2018; see also Chapter 5). Moreover, recent literature on machine learning in comment moderation as reviewed in Chapter 5 highlights that comments can be of value in the news production process (e.g., for post-publication fact checking or providing ideas for follow-up stories). Machine learning's potential to efficiently identify users' arguments, personal stories, as well as "meta-comments" (see Chapter 5) could be harnessed to editorially process such comments. Thus, there is a lot of (editorial and economic) potential in user comments that is not yet realized. Furthermore, we think that there is a lot of unrealized potential when it comes to user engagement: Placing more emphasis on community building can be another useful strategy to establish constructive discussion norms in commentary spaces. Committed users can help newsrooms curate user discussions by constructively replying to problematic commenters in derailing debates (exerting "counter speech" or "corrective action"; Ziegele, Naab, & Jost, 2019). However, such a community must be built up and fostered.

Our Integrated Comment Moderation Model (Figure 6.1) proposes collaborative moderation efforts, combining user-driven moderation support, organizational policies and procedures, and innovative automated solutions (e.g., by AI/machine learning tools). The model suggests making the best use of available assets in the moderation process: users, professional news organizations and staff, and cutting-edge technology.

The model in Figure 6.1 is meant to be a general framework that can be customized across news organizations. We don't expect a given organization to adopt all of the practices listed, but rather consider the most appropriate mix of the three moderation assets for encouraging productive commentary in their particular virtual communities of commenters. Existing empirical research suggests the following can be effective strategies for promoting more user engagement and more civil comments (see Chapter 5): *User-driven* reputation economy, along with options to report/flag abusive comments, reply to other commenters, and community building; *organizational policies* that implement pre-/post-moderation protocols, require user registration and/or the disclosure of social cues, and encourage journalist participation in comment spaces; and *automation*—both fully- and semi-automated, supported by machine learning/artificial intelligence.

In the figure, the arrows among user-driven moderation support, organizational policies, and automation suggest that these approaches should inform one another, in a collaborative and iterative process. For example, transparency and information about moderation policies encourages users to participate in moderation by flagging problematic comments (see Chapter 5). Moderation teams can also be supported by constructive discussion norms established and pursued by committed commenters. Moreover, the semi-automated moderation practices discussed in Chapter 5 involve both user-driven and organizational input to inform automated machine learning technology. For instance, user-driven input integrating reputation economy indicators such as reject rates and numbers of replies/flags/likes can help train moderation algorithms. Furthermore, sentiment analyses can help to automatically identify heated debates. Some topics will more likely result in problematic discussions than others (see Chapter 3). When resources for editorial engagement in comments sections are limited, automated solutions can serve as warning systems to make human moderation more efficient. Still, news organizations would do well to consider the various ethical and methodological challenges discussed in Chapter 5 when developing an Integrated Comment Moderation Model.

In addition, we think that it would be a good time to reconsider interfaces. Thinking about how to aggregate and summarize particularly interesting elements in user commentary—such as overall sentiment, main arguments, personal stories, and feedback to the newsroom—is a task worth engaging in when designing automated solutions (e.g., Loosen et al., 2017). If useful elements in user comments are automatically identified and handily bundled, they will more easily be processed and fed into editorial processes. Moreover, it would be an interesting service to share such summaries not only with the comment moderating or editorial staff but also with the end-users on the 'other side': commenters and comment readers.

More applied research in these areas is still needed—particularly regarding the relative effectiveness of various combinations of user-driven moderation support, organizational policies, and automation, as well as how these moderation assets inform one another—and we hope an Integrated Comment Moderation Model provides a framework for generating future research opportunities. In addition, there continue to be many related scientific questions open for empirical research and public debate. For instance, can commenters' behavior be positively impacted by a 'stricter' adherence to journalistic norms such as "objective" reporting by transparently separating "facts" from authors' opinions, as well as more transparency about the news production process in general? Experiments could also investigate in a more controlled setting how commenters react to constructive or positive news in comparison to traditional reporting styles (that are often accused of being too negative). In particular, we see a need for more longitudinal research: Which factors can, in the long run, positively impact communication behavior among commenters, even under circumstances in which social control is less prevalent? In addition, new theoretical concepts, such as "affective publics" introduced by Zizi Papacharissi (2015, 2016), can help us better understand the interplay between sentiment, enabling, mediating and disinhibiting technology, and political action in networked digital public spheres.

Conclusion

As a common thread throughout this book, we characterize user comments in digital journalism as a disruptive form of user engagement with the news. Comments are valued for their potential to encourage public engagement about the important issues and events of the day, but at the same time these conversations are widely criticized for their often uncivil nature. User comments often exhibit users' overtly critical engagement with the media products they consume and with the elite actors they report upon. We think, however, that by doing so, user commentary also reflects some more general tendencies in current societies across the globe—e.g., comments that critically engage with authorities and elites, in combination with an Internet-enabled empowerment to voice and exert pressure without fear of too much social sanctioning, can become quite an explosive mixture. The publicity that ordinary citizens experience when they publish their opinions online puts them into a powerful position—with both productive and alarming consequences alike, as we discussed throughout this book. For instance, we showed that some forms of such engagement are rightfully feared—e.g., the negative impact on journalists' wellbeing and readers' quality perceptions or trust in the news. However, commentary features also make opinion polarization and problematic opinions public, and thus allow civil society to constructively engage with them. As such, online public spaces are more inclusive—although this does not mean that they are lawless places; they also require ownership and engagement.

Unsurprisingly so, user comments are perceived by many as disruptive to the field of journalism, resulting in many news organizations abandoning their commenting features. At the same time, news organizations' moderation practices can be disruptive to the free flow of user discussions. Our goal in proposing an Integrated Comment Moderation Model is to mitigate these disruptions. By employing more complex and multifaceted moderation, news organizations can work to reduce incivility and encourage more productive commentary; integrating users as partners and community norm-formation as an asset in this process can work to break down the power structures that are imposed on users through more traditional organizationally driven moderation techniques. In doing so, an integrated model offers hope for realizing the ideals of truly reciprocal or participatory journalism models.

In conclusion, we recommend taking the task of moderation more seriously. We think that news outlets have to move away from conceptualizing moderation solely as a process of policing, publishing, or banning user-generated content. Moderation should strive to be much more than that; moderators can pose questions or contribute information, they can summarize or mediate results of discussions to participants and newsrooms alike. If we model moderation as more interactive, this of course comes with the investment of resources, a clear concern among news organizations. Thus, integrating both users and automated tools can be useful: Users provide a wealth of data that can inform moderation practices and give users more voice in the process. Bots, for instance, are able to imitate human communication. Such bots could be trained (e.g., to aggregate and mediate) and then be implemented transparently. Experiments would need to show whether such bots can be "accepted" by commenters and thus be able to positively influence the discussion climate. Comment moderation remains a highly experimental field that requires continued systematic analysis and revisions in the quest to curate productive, engaging, and civil comment spaces.

News organizations have the data and access to the field; communication scholars have the empirical and theoretical backdrop; and computer scientists have the know-how of automation for cost reduction. Collectively, we should investigate the effectiveness of an Integrated Comment Moderation Model. Importantly, while automation might support comment moderation's effectiveness, we need to be wary of the potential for these tools to silence commenters, thereby enacting long-standing gatekeeping power structures. If we truly value commenting spaces for their potential to facilitate public engagement and political action, then as we pursue more innovative moderation techniques and other strategies for improving the quality of user comments, we should aim to ensure that these attempts to promote civil discussion do not limit free speech. In doing so, our hope is that the future of user commentary will be less disruptive for users and news organizations alike.

Note

1 The use of an asterisk in search terms produces any results that include the stem word(s), so for instance "comment," "commenting," and "commentary" would all be included in the results.

References

Goodman, E. (2013). Online comment moderation: Emerging best practices. *World Association of Newspapers (WAN-IFRA)*. Retrieved from http://www.wan-ifra.org/reports/2013/10/04/online-comment-moderation-emerging-best-practices

Ksiazek, T. B. (2015). Civil interactivity: How news organizations' commenting policies explain civility and hostility in user comments. *Journal of Broadcasting & Electronic Media, 59*(4), 556–573. doi: 10.1080/08838151.2015.1093487

Ksiazek, T. B. (2018). Commenting on the news: Explaining the degree and quality of user comments on news websites. *Journalism Studies, 19*(5), 650–673. doi: 10.1080/1461670X.2016.1209977

Lewis, S. C., Zamith, R., & Hermida, A. (2013). Content analysis in an era of big data: A hybrid approach to computational and manual methods. *Journal of Broadcasting and Electronic Media, 57*(1), 34–52. doi: 10.1080/08838151.2012.761702

Liu, J., & McLeod, D. M. (2019). Pathways to news commenting and the removal of the comment system on news websites. *Journalism*. Advanced Online Publication. doi: 10.1177/1464884919849954

Loosen, W., Häring, M., Kurtanović, Z., Merten, L., Reimer, J., van Roessel, L., & Maalej, W. (2017). Making sense of user comments: Identifying journalists' requirements for a comment analysis framework. *Studies in Communication and Media, 6*(4), 333–364. doi:10.5771/2192-4007-2017-4-333

Meltzer, K. (2015). Journalistic concern about uncivil political talk in digital news media: Responsibility, credibility, and academic influence. *The International Journal of Press/Politics, 20*(1), 85–107. doi: 10.1177/1940161214558748

Nielsen, C. E. (2012). Newspaper journalists support online comments. *Newspaper Research Journal, 33*(1), 86–100. doi: 10.1177/073953291203300107

Papacharissi, Z. (2015). *Affective publics: Sentiment, technology, and politics*. New York: Oxford University Press.

Papacharissi, Z. (2016). Affective publics and structures of storytelling: Sentiment, events and mediality. *Information, Communication & Society, 19*(3), 307–324.

Pritchard, S. (2016, March 26). The readers' editor on...closing comments below the line. *The Guardian*. Retrieved from https://www.theguardian.com/commentisfree/2016/mar/27/readers-editor-on-closing-com ments-below-line

Quandt, T. (2018). Dark participation. *Media and Communication, 6*(4), 36–48. doi: 10.17645/mac.v6i4.1519

Santana, A. D. (2011). Online readers' comments represent new opinion pipeline. *Newspaper Research Journal, 32*(3), 66–81. doi: 10.1177/073953291103200306

Strauss, A., & Corbin, J. (1990). *Basics of qualitative research*. Newbury Park: Sage.

Wolfgang, J. D. (2018). Cleaning up the "fetid swamp:" Examining how journalists construct policies and practices for moderating comments. *Digital Journalism, 6*(1), 21–40. doi: 10.1080/21670811.2017.1343090

Ziegele, M., & Jost, P. B. (2016). Not funny? The effects of factual versus sarcastic journalistic responses to uncivil user comments. *Communication Research*. Advance online publication. doi: 10.1177/0093650216671854

Ziegele, M., Jost, P., Bormann, M., & Heinbach, D. (2018). Journalistic counter-voices in comment sections: Patterns, determinants, and potential consequences of interactive moderation of uncivil user comments. *Studies in Communication and Media, 7*(4), 525–554. doi: 10.5771/2192-4007-2018-4-525

Ziegele, M., Naab, T. K., & Jost, P. (2019). Lonely together? Identifying the determinants of collective corrective action against uncivil comments. *New Media & Society*. Advance online publication. doi: 1461444819870130

Index

Note: **Bold** page numbers refer to tables

For Product Safety Concerns and Information please contact our EU
representative GPSR@taylorandfrancis.com
Taylor & Francis Verlag GmbH, Kaufingerstraße 24, 80331 München, Germany

www.ingramcontent.com/pod-product-compliance
Lightning Source LLC
Chambersburg PA
CBHW071054280326
41928CB00050B/2504